AF877363

TAOBAO TECHNOLOGY

www.royalcollins.com

TAOBAO

TECHNOLOGY

ZHAO CHAO

RC

Books Beyond Boundaries

ROYAL COLLINS

TAOBAO TECHNOLOGY

Zhao Chao

First English Edition 2019
By Royal Collins Publishing Group Inc.
BKM ROYALCOLLINS PUBLISHERS PRIVATE LIMITED
www.royalcollins.com

Headquarters: 550-555 boul. René-Lévesque O Montréal (Québec) H2Z1B1 Canada
India office: 805 Hemkunt House, 8th Floor, Rajendra Place, New Delhi 110 008

ISBN: 978-0-9918338-1-8

We are grateful B&R Book Program for the financial assistance in the publication of this book.

Contents

TAOBAO TECHNOLOGY

Preface

This is an interesting book. The first two chapters are mainly about stories, the middle ones about technology, and the last two about people. I posted some of the content found here on my personal blog, and the way it was received among my readers was varied. Some said it was inspiring, while others believed it provided an insight into technology, or was helpful to improving their products, or useful for business start-ups, and some even found the content amusing. That makes it difficult for me to define the book as a book about people or as a book about technology.

Actually, technology books tend to be dull, and I did not mean to put it into this category at the very beginning. Initially, I wrote it for myself. At the end of 2011, I suddenly realized that I had already worked for seven years at Taobao, neither too long nor too short of a time. Some of the stories were as fresh as yesterday, while others were blurred by time. In order to record something for the future, I started to write them down. As so many interesting things happened in these seven years, the more I wrote, the more I wanted to explore. When I started writing this book, I was the Principal of Taobao Technology University, which offered me a great advantage for my writing, since I was able to hear all the stories concerning technology in Taobao from different people. Then I started to write down the technological progress of Taobao in the past few years and then verified the details with the people involved. As some of them had a rather long story to tell, I singled out the conversations with them and present it to the readers in the name of "Collective Biographies of 'Great P's'" (the technical staff of Taobao are defined by P levels, with the "great P's" being specialists with high rankings). This book, therefore, consists of three types of content: my personal experience and the good times I had, the development of Taobao technology, and stories of some legendary people. I hope that the readers will have an understanding of Taobao technology and therefore get a glimpse at the Internet technology through the development of Taobao.

The name of the book—*Taobao Technology*—seems to be too big and bold. But I find it difficult to summarize the content with a more proper name. It is hard to tell the changes in technology at Taobao over ten years in one single book, so I didn't write too much about those fields I was not very familiar with, for instance, operations and maintenance, cloud computing, and big data. This book focuses mainly on the relations between the business of the website and the system structure. I hope it will serve as a modest incentive to spur others to write *Taobao Operation and Maintenance*, and *Taobao Data*, and so on…

I came to realize that I had experienced a great revolution when I read through the book after completing the writing. E-commerce has been pushed in our era to the peak of a great wave, in which I myself am just a little water-drop. I do not intend to describe this big wave, but hope to reflect the stories in the wave through the perspective of a water-drop. This is not an official history of Taobao, for I do not stand so high and have such a perspective. This book is just what a small potato has on his mind.

This book was completed in about 3 months, during which I mainly wrote freely about my own experience, talking about business and technology. I started writing in late 2011 and by early 2012, I had already finished the main body of the book. Next, I had to verify the details, which was a much more tedious job than the initial draft. I interviewed almost everyone mentioned in the book and sometimes I asked some of them to give some supplementary information. As too many were involved, I will not list all your names here but I want to express my gratitude to every one of you, for this is the work of us all.

My special thanks go to my master Yue Xuqiang, who joined Taobao before me. The timeline of this book is based on the stories he told me. Now he has started his own business, and become the CTO of mogujie.com. His leaving Taobao was one of the reasons that I wrote this book. It seems to be only too natural that a company always remains the same, even though there are people coming and going. Although the employee turnover in Taobao has been relatively low in general, once an employee leaves, his or her story also disappears. If I don't tell the stories now, it may be hard for me to present all of them in the future. I chose to write about technologies, to write something about the development of Taobao, and how I came to be the Principal of Taobao University, and therefore, I naturally became the one to tell the stories to the readers.

My gratitude goes to my wife, who made the greatest contribution to the completion of this book. The stories I told in the book were those I told in the classes of Taobao Technology University. But the first listener of each of them was not the technical staff or employees of Taobao. It was my wife, CEO of our family. She acted as a student and listened to my class for more than one hour each time, after which she always pointed out the problems in my narration. In addition, she relieved me from much housework so as to allow me to do the writing freely. Thank you, my dear.

Last but not least, I would like to thank the editor of this book, Mr. Zhang Chunyu who spent a lot of time and energy in the revision of the book. With his help, the book evolved into a real book from just some online articles. Though this book has been revised many times by the writer and editor, it is still possible to find out some bugs, just when software is put online after development. Please do not hesitate to give your suggestions and comments if there are any mistakes.

Ziliu@Hangzhou
April 1, 2013

CHAPTER 1

Personal Website

What technologies does it take to establish a small website? How to take the first step for a website in the context of fierce competition? How did Taobao's unique culture and values come into being? You find the answers in this chapter.

- **The LAMP-based Website**
- **The Origin of Taobao's Swordsmanship and Handstand Cultures**

On April 7, 2003, Ma Yun set up a mysterious organization in Hangzhou. He gathered ten employees, asking them to sign an agreement, which required them to leave Alibaba Group immediately to do a mysterious project which must be kept extremely secret. Ma joked, "You can't even mention it in your dreams in case your wives may hear about it. I'll hunt down anyone who gives it away." The agreement was written in English. Most people signed it in haste without understanding its terms, but, with their trust in Ma, they all left Alibaba straight away.

They went to a mysterious base — an unfurnished house in the estate of Lakeside Garden. The house was owned by Ma Yun. When the small group of people first moved in, Ma Yun gave them an assignment — setting up a C2C (consumer to consumer) transaction website within the shortest time. Here's a question for you to see whether you're qualified to be a member of Taobao's entrepreneurial team: what will you do if it's in your hands?

Before uncovering the answer, I'll first introduce the members of this team: three development engineers (Xuzhu, Sanfeng, and Duolong — these nicknames come from the fictional characters in Chinese swordsman novels), one UED engineer (nicknamed Second Master), three operation engineers (Xiaobao, Ake, and Potian), one manager (God of Wealth), Ma Yun, and his secretary.

The LAMP-based Website

Back then, the biggest pressure for the project team came from time. Why did time matter so much? Master Fire Cloud (a fictional character in a Chinese swordsman novel) once said, "All kinds of martial arts can be cracked except the fast ones." Another reason was that eBay and EachNet were competing fiercely in the capital field, and we were taking the advantage which tended to be easily lost once they realized what we were doing. How to set up a website from scratch in the shortest time? Those who have some knowledge of Taobao's history may know that Taobao was launched on May 10, 2003. It was only a month between April 7 and May 10 of 2003. What would you have done if you had been in this team? We chose to buy a website instead of copying one.

Obviously, buying a website is easier than establishing one from scratch. Yet their dream wasn't just creating a small website but a big one. It couldn't be done by buying a random website. It should have low maintenance costs, convenient for expansion and enhancement maintenance. Then the second question: what kind of website should we buy? The answer was a light and simple one. So we bought a website with such a structure: LAMP (Linux + Apache + MySQL + PHP), which is currently still a frequently-used model for the framework of a website. It enjoys several advantages: no compiling is needed; publication can be made quickly; the PHP language is so powerful that it can do all things from page rendering to data visit; and all the technologies adopted are free, from open sources.

Back then we bought a website system from an American, named PHPAuction (Its official website is http://www.phpauction.net. The name is quite straightforward. You can see what language is used to make this system and what it is for at first sight). PHPAuction has a few versions, and we bought the most advanced one with plenty of functions. Most importantly, we were provided with the source code. The most advanced version was expensive, costing us almost US$2,000 (The price seems to have been lowered to only US$946. Prices are clearly listed on their website.) It couldn't be used straight away after we bought it. Many changes had to be made to localize it, such as changing some data types, increasing the function of background management, improving the page template to make it look nicer, adding the website introduction to the header and footer, and other changes. Of all these jobs, the one that required the highest level of technology caliber was a change made to the database. Originally, all the actions of reading and writing had to be done from one database. We separated the one database into a primary database and two standby ones, with reading and writing detached. In this way, the storage capacity increased; the backup made the website safer; the detachment of reading and writing allowed reading and writing to be done more efficiently (writing consumes more resources than reading and the detachment allowed them to be accomplished independently). The following picture is the structure of the entire system.

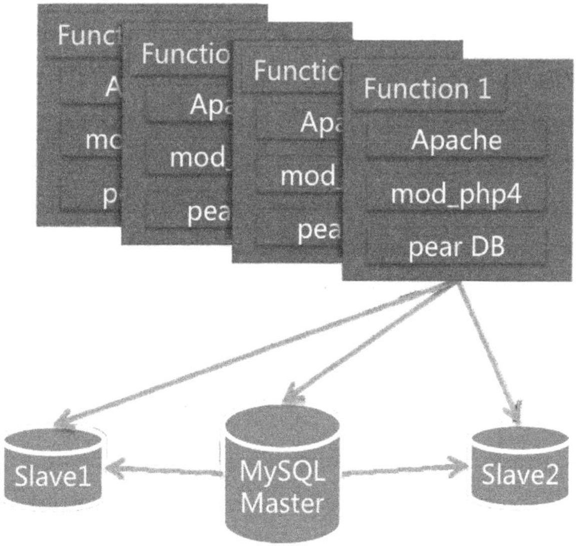

Pear DB in the picture is a PHP module, responsible for the data access layer. In addition, they also used the open-source BBS PHPBB (http://www.phpbbchina.com) to set up a small BBS community. Back then, BBS was a standard part of almost every website. Xuzhu took charge of purchasing machines, configuration, and setting up, etc., while Sanfeng and Duolong coding. They built a channel to connect the user information of the transaction system with that of BBS, developed the background management function (Admin system) for operation staff, and increased three transaction types to the original auction — fixed price, products to buy, and poster products (posters are put up before products are released, which is a great way to quickly increase the number of products). (In the system of PHPAuction, there is only auction. @_行癫 *said in his Weibo: Today, of all the eBay transactions, those done by auction still account for 40%. But in Taobao, this type of transactions has never gained a competitive edge since the beginning, and can almost be ignored in today's mainstream transactions. The reason behind it has been puzzling. I can probably give one of the explanations. EBay's business is usually done in developed countries. After the outsourcing of manufacturing, the basic population of e-commerce is found to be made up of scattered individuals.*)

In the process of development, the code of this project was BMW (right! It means the car exactly). It was proposed by Second Master who's a great fan of the car. He hoped that our website could be as beautiful, fast, safe, and enjoyable as the car. The present personal vehicle of Second Master is a BMW X5. He has finally realized his dream. Before the website was established, it had to be given a name. To avoid the attention of eBay, the name should have nothing to do with Alibaba. So, the domain names like Ali-grandpa and Ali-uncle couldn't be used. At the moment, Ake, the beauty, offered a great name "Taobao". Someone in her family loves to collect antiques and often goes to markets to search for valuable things. She herself loves shopping too. She enjoys the fun of searching for good things. She thought the name "Taobao (search for treasures)" was just right for the website. (Ake said a lightning flashed in her mind the moment she thought of this name. It was indeed an enlightening moment. Later the name of "ZhifuBao (Alipay)" was given by Ake too. So, the name was fixed down and Taobao came into being.

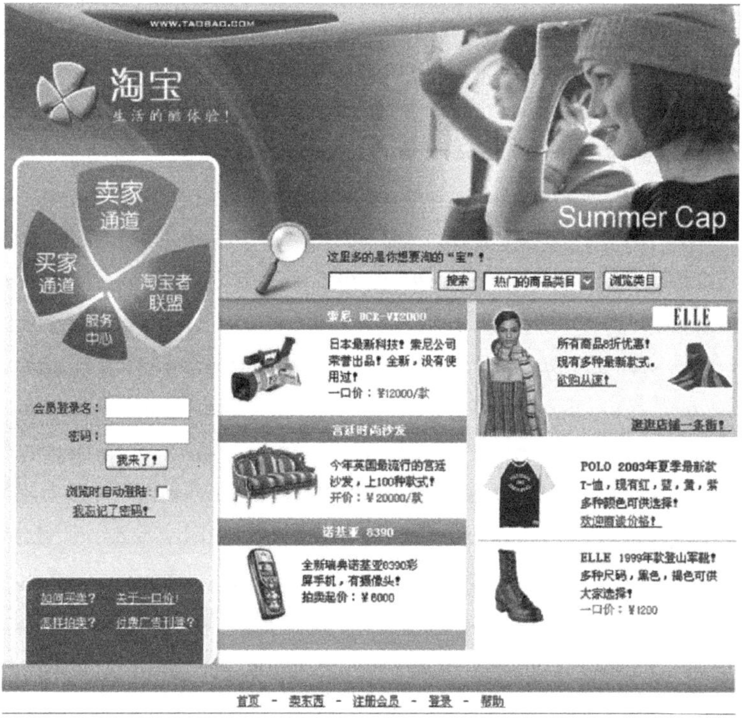

In the better part of the next half year, this website quickly showed its vitality. Here I have to mention the then market situation. The raging SARS (Severe Acute Respiratory Syndrome) threatened everyone who dared to go out, especially to markets where there was usually a dense population. Besides, EachNet, the first C2C website that appeared in China, was busy with big deals at that time.

In March 2002, eBay purchased 33% of EachNet's shares at the cost of USD 30 million. In June 2003, eBAy purchased the remaining 67% of Eachnet's shares with USD 150 million. At that time, Taobao allowed the buyer and the seller of a transaction to leave behind their contact information; same-city transactions were also allowed; the whole process was simple and easy. But you had to pay in eBay. To obtain transaction commissions, eBay forbade buyers and sellers to do so, which inevitably increased the difficulty of the transaction process. Also, for the sake of global unity, eBay replaced EachNet's original system with its American one. All of a sudden, the users had to face an almost new website. It was troublesome to operate on the new system. Many sellers of EachNet couldn't go on. It was like eBay personally gave away its accumulated users to Taobao. In order to avoid the attention of eBay, Taobao claimed to be a "personal website" throughout 2003. Thanks to this founding team's strong marketing and operational abilities, Taobao developed rapidly, attracting 230,000 registered users by the end of 2003, seeing 310,000 PV every day. Between May 2003 and the end of that year, Taobao's turnover value reached RMB 33.71 million. It didn't draw the attention of eBay, but many employees of Alibaba began to notice Taobao's existence. They thought this website would become Alibaba's powerful rival in the future. Some of them even posted on Alibaba's website warning the managing staff against the new website, but the managing staff seemed to pay no attention. (This team really did a great job in keeping it secret!)

The Origin of Taobao's Swordsmanship and Handstand Cultures

Behind the marketing staff and the operation staff, Taobao's technology team was also improving the systems and making innovations rapidly. There's an interesting story about it. In the early period, both eBay and EachNet's employees responded to users' needs on BBS. On eBay's BBS, their employees' words were displayed on a pink background, while the nicknames of EachNet's employees were all related to beans, such as "Soybean", "Broad Bean" and "Black-eyed Bean". This issue was brought forward too when Taobao was discussing the operation strategies. Ma required all the employees to answer the users' questions on the BBS too. At first, the task of answering users' questions was given to Xiaobao. What names should we use? "Taotao," "Baobao," "Tao Baobao," "Baobao Tao"? None of them won Xiaobao's favor. He thought they were too feminine, a humiliation for him, a tall real man. After a long-time discussion, Xiaobao was struck by an inspiration. Why not use the name "Xiaobao (a fictional character)"? Xiaobao and his seven wives opened a shop to welcome the guests' arrival. It reminds you of the story and gives you a real-scene picture. Then many fictional characters in Chinese swordsmanship novels began to pop out and help on Taobao's BBS. Under these nicknames was the mark of "Taobao's Waiter." They answered all kinds of questions and quickly responded to users' various needs. If it was a technical problem, the few of them would discuss it at once before conducting development, testing, and launching. The company rent an apartment for them. They lived in the same apartment in an estate beside Lakeside Garden (with separate rooms for boys and girls). They went to the company when they got up and came back to sleep at 2 or 3 o'clock in the early morning. They could quickly respond to the users' needs. In contrast, after EachNet was purchased by eBay, their system was replaced by the global version. A response to the users' need had to pass multiple approvals. It is said that even the application of buying an office table took two months to be approved. So, their response slowed down naturally.

The system of Taobao's first version already included the functions of product launching, management, searching, product detail, offering to buy, comments and complaints, My Taobao, and others (the present main process consists of these modules too. In October 2003, another function node was added—"Security Transaction", and that was the prototype of Alipay). With the constant growth of user demands and the website flow, many routine changes were made with the system; the number of servers increased from one to three, one for sending Emails, one for database operation, and one for WebApp operation. Later, the function of product searching began to occupy too much space of the databases (the searching function through "like" was very slow). In July 2003, Duolong moved iSearch, the search engine of Alibaba's Chinese station, to Taobao.

Working at such a fast pace, everyone was very exhausted. Someone proposed to do exercise anytime and anywhere. But with that SARS epidemic, how to do exercise in an apartment of over 100 square meters? Tall and pretty Ake suggested doing the hip-lifting exercise, saying it helped to keep a good figure. The suggestion was opposed by all men. Later Xuzhu taught them to do handstand, which was accepted by everyone. And the handstand tradition has been passed down to the present, together with the nickname culture and the swordsmanship culture.

With the soaring of visits and data, problems sprang up soon. The first problem appeared in the databases. The MySQL used then was the fourth version. We used the default storage engine MyISAM, which could lock the table during data writing. When Master synchronized data to Slave, it might cause Slave writing. Thus, Slave's reading action had to wait too. Another problem was the primary key conflict that might happen to Slave, which often led to the halt of synchronization. Then, you wouldn't be able to query what had been definitely published successfully. Besides, the then MySQL wasn't as good as the present one, with plenty of innate shortages in data capacity and security too (compared with Oracle).

CHAPTER 2

Upgrade of the Personal Website

Small websites always wish to scale up in spite of growing pains. What problems did Taobao meet in its adolescence? What concepts did the engineers of Taobao draw on to solve these problems? What innovative approaches did they adopt to surpass their rivals after solving the problems?

- **Database Evolution — from mySQL to Oracle**
- **Innovation of the Payment Method — Alipay**
- **Innovation of Communication — Taobao Wangwang**

By the way, here I need to dispel quite a few widespread on-line rumors first, namely some false inspirational stories to hoax forwarding: "In 1998,Ma Huateng and his partners raised RMB 500,000 to found Tencent and they did not buy a house. In 1998, Shi Yuzhu borrowed RMB 500,000 to develop and promote Nao Baijin (a melatonin product) and he did not buy a house. In 1999, Ding Lei founded 163.com with RMB 500,000 instead of buying a house. In 1999, Chen Tianqiao earned RMB 500,000 through an investment in the stock market and he established Shanda; he did not buy a house. Also in 1999, Ma Yun worked together with his 17 partners to raise RMB 500,000 and registered Alibaba;they did not use the money to buy a house, either. Had these people bought a house with the RMB 500,000, they might be paying the bank loans even today." As a matter of fact, Alibaba and Taobao were established in Ma Yun's apartment, and the website of Alibaba was launched publicly in early 1999. So this is the truth of Ma Yun's house buying.

Taobao as a personal website does not have a long history, but it has kept a high profile. In July 2003, Ma Yun announced that Taobao was a site under Alibaba and then he took exceptionally successful approaches to website promotion and operation in the market. The most notable one is that Taobao made advertisements on small and medium websites so as to break out of eBay's blockage of Taobao's advertisements at portal websites. It was also at that moment that eBay laid eyes on this emerging rival and took the action to "block and put it out." eBay bought out the e-commerce advertisement from Sina, Sohu, and Netease and signed exclusivity agreements to cut off Taobao's efforts to put on advertisements on these sites. Since the road traveled by most people was cut off, Taobao had to search for a new path. People who began to use the Internet at an earlier time should still remember the flashing advertisements on the pop-ups at the right bottom of the web-page and the girdle of the site. The three characters "淘宝网" ("Taobao" in Chinese)were always showing up on those small and medium-sized websites. The guy in the Marketing Department who responsible for buying advertisements was such a spendthrift that as often as not he would spend several million RMB doing his business. As a result, he got a nickname "the Young Master."

Database Evolution — from mySQL to Oracle

Thanks to the Young Master's incessant efforts to put on advertisements, both traffic and transactions of Taobao grew rapidly. However, by the end of 2003, MySQL was no longer able to sustain such a huge volume of traffic. Fortunately the technology replacement was quite simple, and we just evolved to Oracle. The reason why we made this change was that it was of large capacity, stable, safe, and gave an outstanding performance. But most important of all, it was because of our talented team. As early as 2003, Alibaba had already established a powerful DBA team, with big names like Lu Guoliang, Feng Chunpei, Wanghai (nicknamed Qigong, after a fictional character from Jin Yong's wuxia (martial arts) novels, and who is the Beggar Sect chief and a happy-go-lucky guy uses his superb fighting skills to help those in need and perform chivalrous deeds), Feng Dahui (@ fenng) and Chen Jiping (nicknamed Tolui). How awesome are these guys? It is known that Oracle will grant titles to technology experts worldwide. Top class experts are ACES (the same as the top card in the poker game), and now there are only about 300 people in the world who are granted this title Back in 2003, there were only a dozen experts with this honor across the globe, and Alibaba had 4 of them. Equipped with such a powerful technical support, it was only natural for Alibaba to change from MySQL into Oracle.

Of course, to change your database is more than a matter of changing your library. The access and grammar of SQL have to be changed, too. The most important thing is that why the performance and the capacity of the concurrent access of Oracle are so great is due to the critical design of the connection pool. Since there is a long-term connection at the process level in the connection pool, it has to occupy some of the memory space when a process is created. That is to say, these connections are limited on the Oracle Server with fixed memory. Any inquiry only needs to acquire a connection from the connection pool and will be released after use. In this way, it is not necessary to frequently create a connection and disconnect it, for which the cost is tremendous. Given that PHP applied by us has very direct access to the database and each of its inquiries follows a connection. If it is in need of a long connection, when the number of servers increases,that of the connections will accordingly become larger. So the database will be likely to go down under such conditions. In case of short connections, performance will become very poor upon disconnection after frequent connection (On the contrary, Java as a programming language has many existing connection pools). What could we do under these circumstances? At that time, we found out that eBay applied a tool of connection pools sold by BEA. But we also knew that all BEA products were too expensive for us, so we gave up buying to BEA. Then after searching all over the Internet, one of our guys, nicknamed Duolong, found SQL Relay, an open-source connection pool proxy service (http://sqlrelay.sourceforge.net), which could provide the functionality of a connection pool. After Duolong had made some improvements of its functions, the architecture of the system took the form as follows:

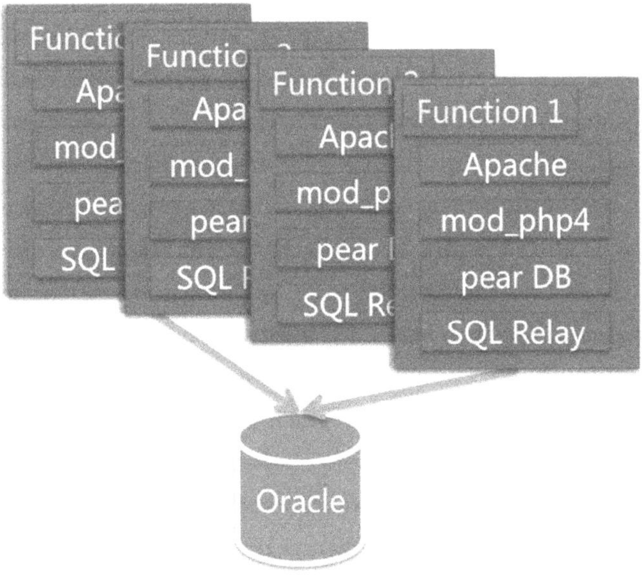

The data was stored locally at the beginning, and the DBA team led by Qigong adjusted and optimized Oracle and SQL. As the volume of data increased, the local storage was no longer able to meet the requirements. The team purchased NAS (Network Attached Storage) from NetApp (Network Appliance) as the storage device and Oracle RAC (Real Application Clusters) to fulfill the load balance. However, Qigong later recalled that the team actually detoured to some extent at that stage since the protocol transmission of the NFS (Network File System) of NAS had severe delays, and nobody knew this. Later the team bought the SAN low-end storage developed by Dell and EMC, which boosted the performance by a dozen times and achieved stable operation. But the data kept growing, RAC went down again with the storage nodes splitting into two and then two into four. We had to resort to minicomputers. That was a turbulent period when Qigong even stayed five days and nights in the company's computer room. We were so worried that he might get enough radiation to become a mutant like Spider Man.

It was spring of 2004, after the replacement of database was done. There was a saying that "night hours in spring are extremely precious." But the nights for those DBA team members were rather tough. They kept encountering bad luck after the data connections were placed to the SQL Relay. The service was often deadlocked, just the same deadlock situation as when MySQL was used. Despite many corrections made by Duolong, the logic of internal processing for the version at that time was not correct and thus had many problems. Hence the last solution was to reboot the service. Rebooting was tolerable in the daytime. All that the technicians needed to do was to get it connected with the servers in the computer room, kill the process and reboot it. The hardest moment was when the connections also went down during nighttime. Engineers had to keep their mobile on 7/24 so that they could be woken up by the alert message "the SQL Relay process is hung;" then they would turn on the computer, get it connected with the network of the computer room and reboot the service. Later all engineers would reboot before going to bed every night. It was said that the guy who did the most rebooting was Sanfeng, current President of Taobao. Now we can conclude that every genius must have undergone an extremely hard time before they become a genius.

Innovation of the Payment Method— Alipay

There is an opinion on Weibo that "a good architecture is the result of evolution instead of design." It is true and we may consummate it by adding"so is a good function." In the process of the architecture growth, Taobao business also developed rapidly. At an early stage, the buyer transferred money via their bank account to the seller after placing an order on Taobao. However, some dishonest sellers refused to deliver the goods after receiving the money and finally just disappeared. It was very serious and the fear was that, like a virus, others may follow suit. But Taobao people began to study the solutions on how to prevent fraud. Firstly they tested using PayPal to accept payments, but found it impossible to solve the problem. Then they saw to something similar to Q-coins and tried to create Taobao coins, but they still could not prevent fraud from happening. Finally, these bright minds came together to collect all ideas and brainstorm. Then they came up with the idea of a secured transaction, a third-party fund trusteeship. Hence in October 2003, Taobao released a new function named Safe Transaction. If a seller chooses to apply the function, the buyer would first pay to Taobao and then Taobao would transfer the amount to the seller after the buyer received the goods. Safe Transaction was the prototype of Alipay. The function was initially an option to sellers as the cycle of payment receipt would be delayed if they choose it. But once the sellers applied the function, they found surging transactions. Only one year later, almost every seller turned to the secured transaction. Later it was a must for all transactions to follow the Safe Transaction mode. On the annual conference of Alipay in 2012, the transactions published by Alipay doubled those completed through PayPal. Such an epic innovation actually came into being from a burst of clarity after incessant exploration.

The developers of the Safe Transaction were Mao Shiba and Miao Renfeng—his disciple (these are their nicknames adapted from wuxia novels).

Mao Shiba went to Shanghai to pursue an MBA degree in the middle of the development of Safe Transaction, while Miao Renfeng is now Chief Business Architect of Alipay). Duolong was in charge of developing the function to join the gateway of the banks. It seemed that at that time most bank websites supported the on-line payment. But Duolong told me that their gateways and technologies were so diversified that we in Taobao had to join them one by one. In addition, there was no guarantee that the bank gateway would successfully deduct the amount after the user made a payment, or that Taobao would be notified after a successful payment deduction, or the notification to Taobao would be 100% successful or that there would be no repeated notification after the notification had already arrived. So many "no-guarantees" put Miao Renfeng in a bind. He had to reconcile accounts with statements manually every day and could not sleep well if even a penny was lost; as that meant somebody could not find his/her money, which would be a big problem. In order to test the functions of these gateways, he also went to all the banks in Hangzhou to apply for a card, resulting in a large pile of cards on his desk. The people who did not know the background thought Miao Renfeng must be a rich guy. Actually, the balance in each card was normally between RMB 8 and RMB 10. We see again the suffering behind each genius..

Innovation of Communication — Taobao Wangwang

Someone said that the reason why Taobao could beat Eachnet (then eBay China) was that Taobao applied the free-of-charge strategy. But this was only one of the reasons. If free-of-charge is the first step taken by Taobao, in its rivalry against Eachnet (which offered free listings for users), then the second step was Safe Payment, so that users may rest assured after making a payment and have no worry of being cheated. In popular Chinese wuxia novels, true martial masters may even hurt their opponent by lightly throwing a flower or a leaf. They have multiple unique kill shots and when fighting, they will make continuous shots. The third unique shot of Taobao was Wangwang. Taobao Wangwang was a replication of Alibaba's Maoyitong (now merged with Taobao Wangwang). In March 2004, the classic sound "Ding-dong, Ding-dong" began to echo in the ears of all Taobao buyers and sellers. "Dear, is delivery free?" "Dear, could the price be RMB 0.5 lower?" Such friendly bargaining later developed into the famous Taobao Style. Chinese people are said to love a bargain, although I myself do not feel a sense of accomplishment after a successful bargaining. I am made to see the true value of Taobao Wangwang in trading every time I go to the food market and see middle-aged women bargaining with great enthusiasm and feel so happy that they seem to have gotten a bargain. I suppose that eBay can not be able to sense the fun of bargaining, as they do not allow sellers and buyers to chat on-line all the way. Even after buying Skype, eBay did not apply it to e-commerce.

But we did not expect a legal dispute after Wangwang was launched. A rice cracker maker named Wangwang came to us and said we infringed upon their name They produced delicious rice crackers and quality milk, which were popular in China and enjoyed by all of us. So we added two words in front of Wangwang to make it Taobao Wangwang, in order to calm the waters. There was only one developer of Wangwang in the earliest stage, a guy nicknamed Wu Yazi. He is the "Father of Wangwang" in our eyes. In order to support him, the IM tool we used at work was only limited to Wangwang. When the on-line numbers of Wangwang hit new records, he would buy us spicy duck necks (a kind of tasty Chinese snack). Hence sometimes we just looked closely at the on-line numbers, and logged on with our alternate IDs when another new whole number came out so that we may enjoy one more feast of duck necks. When it comes to Wangwang, we should not forget mentioning another lovely designer, a girl named Qi Ling. It was she who developed the whole set of Wangwang emojis. These emojis, which are bigger and more vivid compared with the same of all other chat software, are still being used today. Qi Ling is our "Mother of Wangwang."

In that stage of wild growth, we developed whatever we could imagine, and a lot of products came into being during that period. For example, we even built a chat room. However it seemed that

Taobao was not a place for chatting. Therefore the chat room gained little popularity. We had to shut it down a short time later.

Let us return to the topic of SQL Relay. As the issues with SQL Relay persisted, the team of Sanfeng was hard put to have a complete and sound sleep. On the semi-annual conference that year, the company presented Sanfeng an award as an appreciation for his team's great efforts. But you could never maintain the stability through around-the-clock rebooting. As a result, at the beginning of the first half of 2004, we began to conduct a complete transformation of the whole website.

CHAPTER 3

An Enterprise-level Java Site

It would be enough to make one shudder to only think of changing the programming language of a website. However, Taobao accomplished this by changing from PHP to Java in 2004. How did it do it? To what architecture should an enterprise-level Java system apply? The challenges faced by a site could be mainly summarized as performance, capacity, and cost. Is there a common solution to these issues? With the improvement of technology, in which fields do we see a spectacular growth of Taobao's business? Still which businesses would meet technical obstacles?

- **A Radical Upgrade — Change of Programming Language**
- **Harder than a Rock — Evolution of Performance, Capacity, and Cost**

Huang Shang, my master, once said that "A good architecture chart is an expression of great beauty." We could tell if an architecture is good or not just from the aesthetic perspective. I found this viewpoint basically true after having studied quite a few system architectures. If we look at the two versions of Taobao architecture displayed in the following chart, which one appears more pleasant to you?

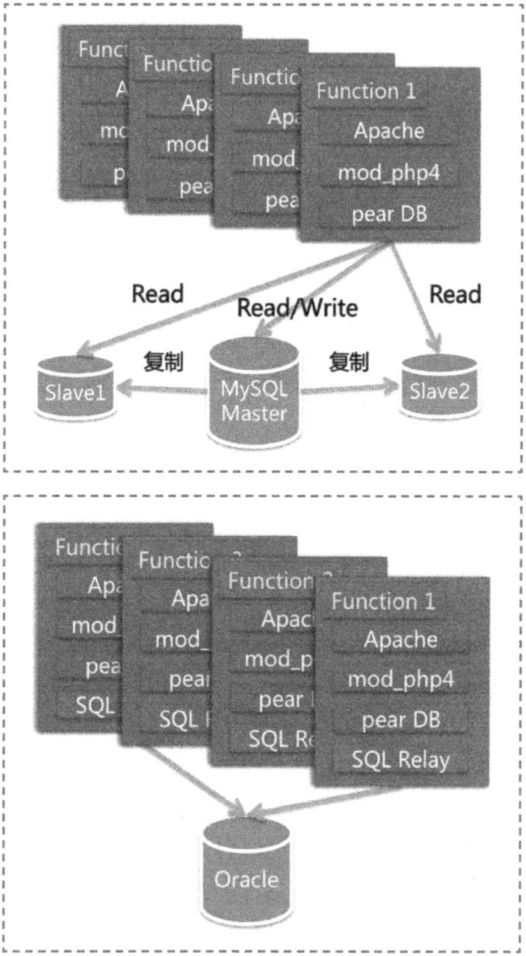

Apparently the first one is more attractive, while the second one, which seems top-heavy, was destined to be unstable and in fact only survived for less than half a year. In early 2004, the issues with SQL Relay persisted, and it was a must to change it to Oracle. Where should we begin then? The only solution was to change the programming language. And what language should we apply? Java. As the most sophisticated web development language at that time, Java boasted a sound enterprise development framework and was generally adopted by the mainstream large scale websites around the world. In addition, there were plenty of talent programmers with a certain experience in Java development and the cost was low for follow-up repair and maintenance.

A Radical Upgrade — Change of the Programming Language

Until the first half of 2004, Taobao had operated for a year, accumulating a large number of users, while quickly developing many functions. The site at that time was enormous, while new demands kept increasing. It was nothing less than a matter of reshaping a big website to change its programming language while the development of business was not allowed to slow down. The change in the process of operations posed great challenges in terms of time and technology. If we compared to the change to a medical operation, it was a must to invite first-class surgeons to perform the surgery. Now we also have a question for everyone:

Dear all, what kind of people would you like to invite in a start-up team?

Our answer was to invite the people from the Sun Corporation. Yes, it is the company that created Java, for who would know Java better? On top of that, there was a reason that only a few people knew. Just as I mentioned that Java was broadly applied by large, main stream websites, and eBay was one of them. The system of eBay had recently changed from C++ to Java at that time, and they invited engineers of Sun to change the system into the Java architecture. Now did you get my point? The Sun engineers not only knew Java well, they also knew eBay better.

The guys were really something! When I came to Taobao at the end of 2004, they were still in Taobao. It was my good fortune to work with them for a couple of months. At that time, they just faced the issue of how to evolve the programming language of a huge site from PHP to Java. In the meanwhile, they could not shut down the service so that the bug-fix and functions of the original system would not be affected. So if you were the architect, what would you do? Someone's answer was to compile a translator, and then translate the PHP to Java automatically, just like the Chinese-English translation. I have to say that your thought is too cutting-edge and "too young, too simple, sometimes naive." There was nobody capable of compiling a translator at that time, and there is still none even today. The general plan of the Sun people was to divide various modules for different types of business and then gradually replace them module by module. Take the user module as an example. The new functions developed on the new module shared a common database with the old module when the ongoing maintenance was conducted to the old member.taobao.com with no new function being added. The completed development was placed into the various application clusters. Another domain name was opened separately when the old functions were replaced. Each function on the old modules would be shut down when it was replaced so that the users would be guided to member1.taobao.com. The member.taobao.com would be closed finally after all functions had been replaced. In the viewpoint of design, the second-level domain name should be in the transition. However when we logged off the codes of the member domain name, we found it hard to switch from member 1 to member, since some places had hard-coded the links. For a long time thereafter, we had to use the weird domain name member1.taobao.com. A year later, another Internet company started e-commerce and we noticed that their domain names were member1.xx.com and auction1.xx.com. Their complete and unreserved replication made us chuckle.

We just talked about the development mode, now let us discuss the Java MVC framework. At that time the struts1.x was the framework that was frequently applied. But those who have used webwork and struts2 might know that there is an Achilles' heel of struts1.x in terms of multiple-party cooperation. It was hard to extend because there was no lightweight framework as the basis. For this reason, it was rather difficult for architects to have control over the basic functions. Among the 18 founders of Alibaba, there is an architect named Zhou Yuehong who accomplished many extensions on the basis of Jakarta Turbine and created an MVC Framework WebX (http://www.openwebx. org/docs/Webx3_Guide_Book.html) dedicated to Alibaba. The framework was easy for extension and modularization development, whose page template supported JSP and Velocity, persistent layer supported ibatis and hibernate and control layer allowed the application of EJB and Spring (which appeared later). Hence the project team chose this powerful framework. In addition, at that time Sun was vigorously promoting their EJB and firmly insisted that Taobao apply it despite the fact that the architects in Taobao were dubious about its necessity. After many technical discussions, arguments and even conflicts with each other, the architecture of the system is shown in the following chart.

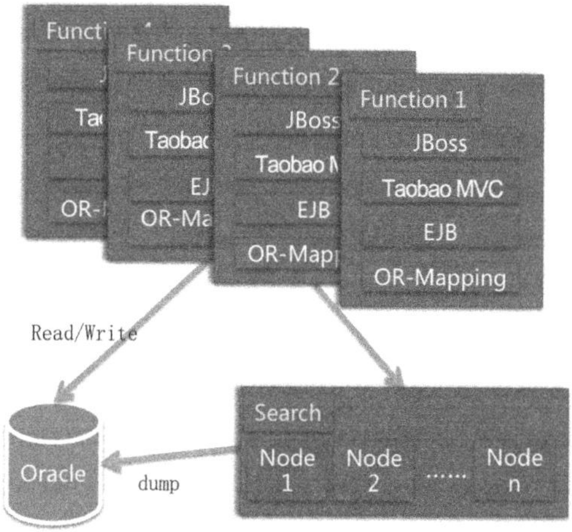

The MVC framework is Alibaba's WebX, the control layer applies EJB while the persistent layer adopts ibatis. On the other hand, the inquiries of commodities and shops are put in the search engine to relieve the stress of the database. Now does the architecture chart look better?

After Sun's engineers had finished the development of Taobao's website, they built a killer site with the same architecture, which is called Alipay. (We have mentioned in the previous chapter that Alipay was originally referred to as the Safe Transaction function, which was later separated out as a site and the foundation of a company, i.e. today's Alipay. The people who split Alipay from Taobao were the guys from Sun.) The following is the picture of the first staff meeting of Alipay.

We introduced the search engine iSearch to the above architecture (As was mentioned earlier, iSearch was introduced by Duolong after the LAMP system had been operating for a while. As the database was replaced by Oracle, only the data source was changed.) The rationale of the search engine is quite simple, which is to dump the data in the database to the structured text files and save them on the hard disks so as to enable the Web applications to inquire about the data with the agreed parameters and grammars. It seemed to be of little difficulty. Actually given that there are hundreds of millions of bits of information, how could we do a fast update? For example, you have a newly established website, and find that you can pinpoint it on Baidu just after three days. You must be very happy with the result, right? However, things would turn out otherwise if you have published a commodity on Taobao but still cannot find it after an hour. That is very frustrating. Another problem we faced was how to ensure a high capacity and large quantity of concurrent connections. After that we needed to consider the issues of segmentation and semantic analysis as well as the more intelligent points such as the recommended algorithms. But these contents will not be discussed in details here as it would take a few books just to cover the technology of the search engine.

In fact at no time has the programming language itself been the bottleneck of the system; pressure brought by the increasing business is more frequently found in data and storage. We have also mentioned earlier that we switched to Oracle after MySQL was no longer capable of supporting the site. The storage of Oracle was on the native machine and then moved to NAS. When NAS was no longer adequate, SAN of EMC was used for storage. At last, when RAC of Oracle was no longer able to work properly, we had to turn to microcomputers for data storage. In the summer of 2004, Qigong of DBA, test engineer Guo Fu, and architect Xing Dian went to Beijing to test microcomputers. When they came back with the equipment, we gave them a grand reception . It was our most valuable equipment and the numbers on the price list were enough to freak people out. Upon the arrival of the microcomputers, we squeezed forward to have a photo with it before Oracle ran on the microcomputer. Storage evolved from the low-end CX storage of EMS to Sun oem hds high-end storage and then to EMC dmx high-end storage, realizing a three-step leap.

At the end of 2004, there were already over 4 million commodities on Taobao with over 40 million PV on an average daily basis, 4 million members registering and RMB 1 billion of turnover across the site.

Up to now, we have applied IBM microcomputers, Oracle databases, EMC storage, all of which were very expensive. Money

just burnt a hole in our pocket in those days. There is a saying that the problem which can be solved with money is not a real problem. With the development of Taobao, before long money was no longer able to solve our problems. The extravagantly priced configuration may be able to support the site with 100 million PV, but given the exponential growth of Taobao, what could we do when there are 1 billion PV? What would happen in case of 10 billion PV? In just a few years, we had to create new technologies to solve the problems that would be encountered by the top world-class sites. Later we started an independent development on the basis of open-source software and gradually removed the once fabulous tools such as IOE (IBM microcomputers, Oracle and EMC storage). These fabulous tools were just like the weapons of immortals in the great Chinese novel, Journey to the West. When the demons, once the servants to the immortals, took these weapons, even the almost all-mighty Monkey King would have to run away, defeated. However, the greatest immortals never rely on these weapons. A flick of the sleeve or overturned palm may be extremely powerful.

Harder than the Rock — Evolving of Performance, Capacity, and Cost

Now our readers might be impatient and eager to know why we got rid of IOE? Let me explain step by step because there was still a long way to go before the removal of IOE (later when we talk about TDDL, there will also be some stories about its removal). We were able to use Oracle immediately after the team led by Xing Dian bought the microcomputer back. Then Qigong led a team of DBA to optimize SQL and storage while Xing Dian led a few architects to study the extendability of the database. But Oracle itself is a closed system. How could it be extended? Let's use a trendy expression to describe our method, i.e. database sharding.

We all know that the processing capability of an Oracle has an upper limit, and the quantity of connection pools is also limited while the inquiry rate is inversely proportional to the capacity. In short, Oracle will meet its extremity when the data volume reaches over 100 million, and the queries exceed 100 million. The simplest approach to break through the limit is to apply more Oracle databases. But since we were going to extend in a closed system, it would not be as easy as adding machines directly to a distributed system. Our approach was saving the user information in two databases (DB1 and DB2) based on IDs, saving information of commodities and sellers in two corresponding databases and then placing the general information such as the category of commodity in the third database (DBcommon). The purpose of doing this, apart from extending the database capacity, was for the sake of disaster recovery. In case one database broke down, at least half of the commodities across the site were available.

But the application got into trouble after we arranged the databases in this way. If I was the seller, it wouldn't be difficult for me to check all my commodities since they were in the same database. However, when it comes to the buyer who bought commodities in both DB1 and DB2, how would the application work if the buyer checked things in "What I Bought?" The buyer had to check the corresponding commodities in two databases. What if the commodities were arranged by the order of the purchase date? We found out all the items in "What I Bought" in both databases to consolidate them in the application. Furthermore, what should we do with the paging? What about the query of key words? If we put it more professionally, that would be like "we could not accomplish the 'Join' of the data". If we assigned the task to the programmers, it would be a big headache to them. So our architect Xing Dian took it over to write a DBRoute, a framework of database route to handle the operations including the consolidation, sorting, and paging of data in a unified method so that the programmers may use the data in multiple databases in the same way as in one database. The framework was still applied after Taobao began to use Oracle. Unfortunately, the second purpose of database sharding — disaster recovery was not brought into reality with the development of business. Many parts such as commentary, compliant, whistle-blowing, collection and My Taobao must connect with DB1 and DB2 simultaneously, so when either of them broke down, the whole site was down.

As we said earlier that EJB was actually the result that we had compromised with the Sun engineers. After they had left, EJB also faded out. Spring acquitted itself brilliantly in 2005 and 2006. So we replaced EJB with Spring and streamlined many of the codes for the overall system.

Again, as we have said previously, we introduced in the search engine with a view to reducing the stress of the database and improving the efficiency of searching. As data kept growing, the pressure of data storage was mounting with the then 16.63 million commodities, 89.31 million PV and 13.90 million registered members. The speed slowed because of the growth of data. Dear all, now let me ask you a new question. Is there any way to improve the system performance besides the search engine and database sharding? Of course, there must be a way. That is cache and Content Distribution Network (CDN).

You can just imagine when the visitors volume reached 90 million, how much of it would be found in the web page of commodity details. When users visited the page, all data were read-only (which were read out from the database without writing in it). Then our master architect Duolong created a cache system based on Berkeley DB and put into it much read-only with few changes. At first, the system was rather weak and we dared not save all cache information in it. We first saved the information of sellers in the system, then the commodity attributes and later the information of shops. However, the fields of the commodity details were too long to save. These fields were horrible, and the statistics showed that the printout of them would run for 5 meters on average. It is no wonder that nobody favored them. I still remember clearly that as a project manager of Taobao, my first project was to move the commodity details from the commodity tables. In the earliest stage, they were saved in the same table with the prices, freight, and other information. Therefore the query rate of the whole list was dragged down while on many occasions, the query of commodity information needed no details. In 2005, I began to move these details to another table in the database, and all of these big character fields were first moved out of the database to the cache system and then to the TFS.

Today the whole pages of commodity details are kept in the cache. Our goggle-eyed readers might find that at present the commodity details are not all "read-only," and there is a "Page View' (which was added in 2006) on the web page. Whenever there is a refresh of the viewing number, the page will be "written" in the storage. Is it possible to apply cache for such highly frequent real-time updates? Generally speaking, they must be saved in the database. But unfortunately in 2006 when we were developing the function to write the views into the database, the database broke down an hour after the function was released. It is totally unbearable for the database to save hundreds of millions of write-ins each day. What should we do? I will keep it a secret for a moment and tell you the answer in the later discussion of the cache Tair. (The following is not an advertisement and please divert your attention from the left, to the middle right and check where the data of page views is.)

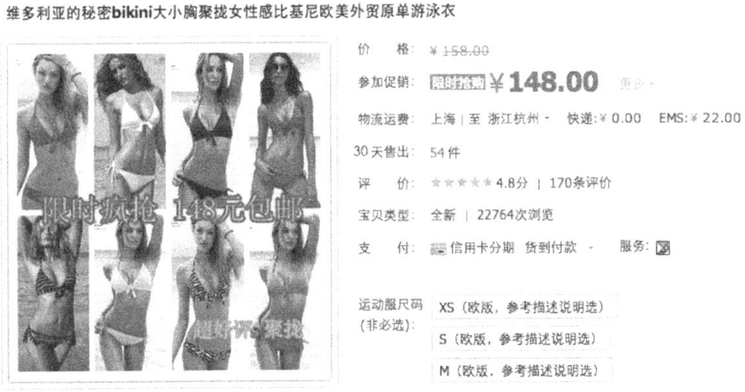

The work of the CDN was relatively independent. Just as with other systems, we applied the commercial ones at the beginning. But it could not work properly with the growing traffic. Dr. Zhang Wensong, founder of LVS, led his guys to build a Taobao CDN network. I have mentioned in chapters above that the Taobao CDN system supported a traffic volume of over 800Gbps. In contrast, we may have a look at the brief of ChinaCache, a listed domestic company dedicated to CDN —"ChinaCache is the top professional CDN service provider in China offering our clients holistic solutions of fast network content distribution. As the first CDN service provider to obtain a permit from the Ministry of Industry and Information Technology of China, ChinaCache now has nearly 300 nodes in over 50 big and medium-sized cities across China with a network-wide processing capacity of over 500Gbps. Its CDN network has covered major operators such as China Telecom, CNC, China Mobile, China Tietong, and CERNET." — the traffic volume of Taobao alone is greater than the total of theirs altogether. Thus you can see the power of Taobao in CDN, which is in the top rank worldwide (the commercial CDN adopted by us first was ChinaCache, and they supported us for a long while.) In addition, as the application of CDN needs a large number of servers, large amount of energy will be consumed (How much is it? Two years ago, we did some computing for this. When there is a transaction occurring on Taobao, the electricity consumed will be enough to boil 4 eggs). Dr. Zhang Wengao's team is studying the low power consumption servers in these two years and has done a lot of creative work in green computing. We also customized low power consumption servers based on the Intel Atom processors of his team and had them deployed in our CDN rooms, resulting in great reduction of energy consumption. You may read about this in my interview with Dr. Zhang.

In retrospect of the period when we first applied the cache, I was still a rookie and often made a common mistake, in that I often forgot to notify the cache system. As a result, when in testing I failed to find any difference on the page of my corrected data. Then I created some codes of pages, but failed to update the user's information cached locally when correcting CSS and JS and led to a messy page. When someone on the forum complained, I would tell him/her to use Ctrl+F5 (to erase the local cache for page refreshing), then correct the name of script files and re-launch the page.

All our actions, such as database sharding, EJB withdrawal, the introduction of Spring, addition of cache, and CDN, were seemingly at random. Actually they were done with our adherence to the purposes of capacity improvement, performance enhancement, and cost saving. As these changes were not drastic, the version after we made these changes was named v 2.1 by us and had only three legs in the chart. But at this point does it look more stable?

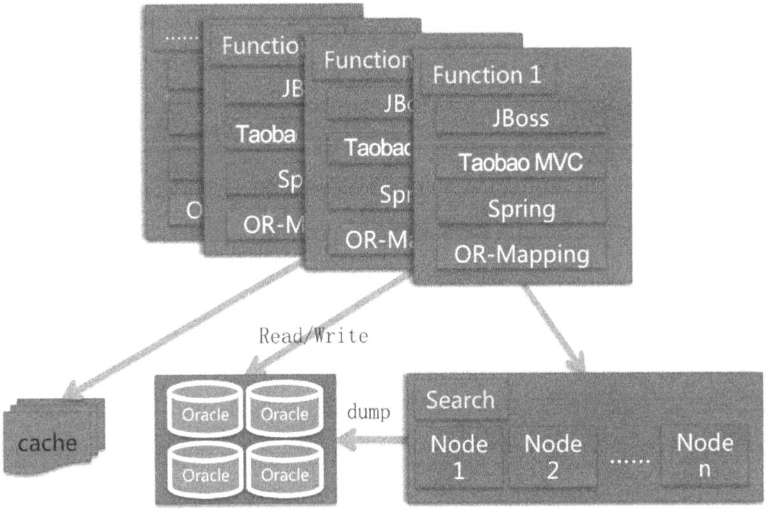

Thanks to this stable version, Taobao's business underwent development by leaps and bounds. When MSN, the portal of Microsoft, made its grand debut in China in May 2005, Taobao joined in as its shopping channel. In the middle of 2005 when Shanda started marching into the field of Set Top Box, Taobao developed its TV shopping functions. Although these two types of business faded gradually due to the local conditions or some policy reasons, they were really big events in the Internet industry of China. The guy negotiating with Microsoft on the cooperation was nicknamed @胖胡斐 Pang Hu Fei, who was also a spendthrift and called Second Master by us. He is now CEO of www.mogujie.com.

In addition, boss Ma never lacked a fun spirit. After watching the huge success of the Super Girl singing contest launched by Hunan Satellite Television, he wanted to copy its mode. Hence at the end of 2005, Taobao and Hunan Satellite Television worked together to launch a program called "Super Buyer Show." Dedicated to selecting a person who is super capable of buying, the show had a lot of buyers share their experience of on-line shopping so that the winner would be selected by online polls to win an annual salary of RMB 1 million. It took more than a year for the program to go through mass auditions and on-stage performance with advertisements being posted everywhere. Although it was less of a blockbuster than the Super Girls, people finally had a deep impression of Taobao—an online shopping website thanks to the promotion by Hunan Satellite Television.

By 2006, Taobao had already had an annual PV volume of 150 million, a total of over 50 million commodities, more than 30 million registered users and turnover of RMB 16.9 billion.

CHAPTER 4

Technology Creation

Problems that can be solved with money are not problems after all. We can use money to buy better machines and better services, but when you become the best of the industry, you'll meet problems that no one else has ever come across before, which means that you'll have to solve the problems by yourself. Taobao has been lucky for its rapid development; but it's also been unlucky for it met unprecedented problems. As a result, the site had no choice but to turn to technological innovations. So, we may pose a question: has tech innovation pushed the advancement of business innovation or the other way round?

- **Taobao File System — TFS**
- **Taobao KV Cache System — Tair**

Let's review the versions mentioned above. Version 1.0 of the PHP system ran for nearly one year (from May 2003 to January 2004), with one server at first and later multiple servers. Then, as the database could no longer meet the demand, we replaced MySQL with Oracle and introduced in the search engine (version 1.1 from January 2004 to May 2004); less than half a year later, the programming language was changed to Java (version 2.0 from February 2004 to March 2005), with IOE adopted gradually for data services; with the increase of data input and page views, we divided the database, added cache, and used CDN (version 2.1 from October 2004 to January 2007). The periods of these versions sometimes overlap as many schema didn't evolve at a particular time but slowly and gradually.

When describing the version 2.1, I used a title "Harder than a Rock" because we finally had a stable version. Taobao operated more than two years on the system of that version. During that period, lots of outstanding people joined in and we developed many excellent products, such as the product category property, Alipay certification system, the project of Wealth Pull, Taobao Travel, Taobao Lottery, and Taobao Forum. And even before the boom of group-buying websites, Taobao already developed the function of group buying as early as in 2006.

At the base of these products and functions are actually two major functions — product management and transaction management. Radical changes in both of the major functions may be found in version 2.1. At first the product management function provided buyers with two options, 7-day expiration and 14-day expiration. Products would be removed off the shelves on the day of expiration and had to be released again to be sold. And the products would have new ID after they were placed on the shelves again. In addition, after a product was sold in that period, new supplies of the same product had to be released with a new ID. There were a few reasons for that: First, it followed the time setting pattern of auctions, where a product could only be listed in a limited period of time; second, the search engine that could not figure out which one of the same products should be placed in the front row usually placed the one with the longest time of being listed in the front row (so, the old products must be removed at a certain time, or it would hang in the front row all the time); third, as the transaction information and the product ID were connected, the product information in the transaction record would constantly change with the seller editing the product information repeatedly if the ID remained the same; another hidden reason was that we didn't have enough storage to allow all the products to be stored in the primary database all the time. This way of management is simple and rough, but also fair enough. However it led to the failure to satisfy many demands. For example, a seller couldn't change the price of a product after it was sold, or the price in the previous transaction would change accordingly. Besides, the favorable comments in the previous transaction couldn't be displayed for the same product. Also, a buyer could only see the transaction information after a product was bought without the knowledge of whether the seller would continue to sell the same product or not. Based on these demands, in the second half of 2006 we separated the product management and the transaction management. One kind of product of a seller had only one ID, whether it had been sold or not. Then how to deal with the information of previous transactions if the seller changed the price of the product, the inventory, or other information? We recorded the snapshot of every transaction. so buyers and sellers were happy about that, but what did it mean for our system? It meant a dramatic increase of storage costs.

Taobao File System — TFS

How high could the storage costs be? We employed IOE for the database. One set of it cost about RMB 12 million, and a few sets of it meant a lot of money. Also, Taobao had numerous other files to be stored, including pictures, item descriptions, and transaction snapshots. Each item contained several pictures and lengthy descriptive information, and several thumbnails of different specifications had to be generated for each picture. In 2010, 28.6 billion images were stored in the back-end system of Taobao. Pictures mean a lot in the transaction system. We often say "a great pic is worth more than a thousand words" and "pics or fake." When it comes to the Taobao site, the pictures of items, shopping-rush items in particular, have colossal page views. Of all the page views of Taobao.com, those of pictures total more than 90%. The average size of the pictures is 17.45KB; the pictures less than 8KB total 61% of all, accounting for 11% of the overall system capacity. The large amount of image data and the huge number of page views posed tough challenges to Taobao. For most systems, the biggest trouble lies in the storage and reading of large quantities of small files as the magnetic heads have to seek and change tracks frequently, which may lead to a long time delay in data reading. The huge number of concurrent visits is the system's nightmare. What should be done?

Similarly, when the size of your business is within a certain limit, you may employ the current business solutions, but when your business goes beyond the limit, the current business solutions won't be able to meet your demands and you have to create your own solutions. For Taobao's image storage, the turning point was in 2007. Prior to that, we had been using a commercial storage system, NetApp's file storage system. With the total number of Taobao's image files tripling every year, Taobao's back-end storage system developed by NetApp was gradually upgraded from the basic version to the advanced one until 2006 when even NetApp's most advanced storage system couldn't meet Taobao's requirements. In 2006, we decided to develop on our own a file system which was dedicated to the storage of a massive number of small files so as to solve the problem of image storage, which marked Taobao's transition from technology adoption to technology creation.

Taobao's image storage architecture prior to 2007 was as follows:

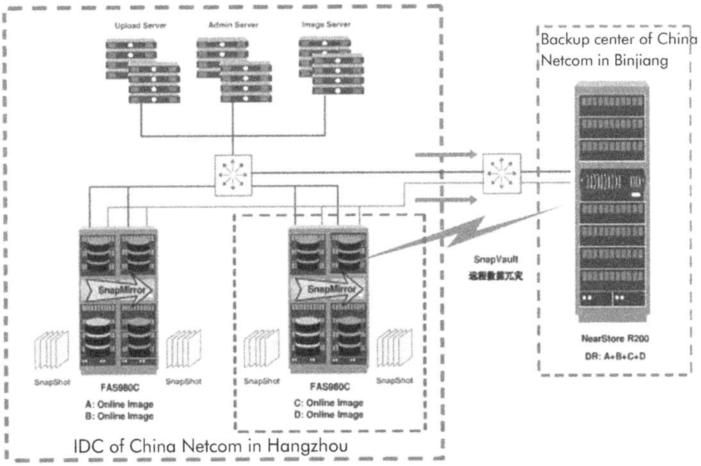

Note: The equipment in the red square was newly added in 2006. It is planned that another 20TB of hard disc capacity will be added to the original NetApp 980C/R200 next year.

At an architect conference, Dr. Zhang Wensong summarized the limitations and disadvantages of a commercial storage system:

First, a commercial storage system didn't have specific optimization regarding the storage and reading environment of small files; second, the online storage facilities couldn't support a large number of files; third, as more and more servers had been connected to the system, the number of network links had reached the limit of the network storage facilities; and fourth, there was a high cost for the capacity expansion of a commercial storage system — the capacity of 10TB would cost several million RMB, and the commercial storage system was plagued with single point failures, which made it hard to ensure good disaster recovery and security.

In a comparison of the economic benefits between a commercial system and a self-developed one, Dr. Zhang set out the following aspects:

First, commercial software was not able to meet the practical requirements of large-scale systems. In a manufacturer's lab, it was almost impossible to realize such a large-scale test of storage, CDN, or load balancing.

Second, in the process of research and development, combining open source with independent development would allow us to have a better control. If the system had a problem, we could certainly solve it at the basic level, and the system would have a better extensibility.

Third, when the business reached a certain size, the investment in research and development would be worthwhile. The following chart shows the input and output ratios of a self-developed system and a commercial system. In fact, on the left of the intersection, a commercial system is always a more practical and more economical choice; only when the business size goes beyond the intersection can a self-developed system generate great economic benefits. In fact, not many companies have reached that size, but Taobao has gone far beyond that intersection.

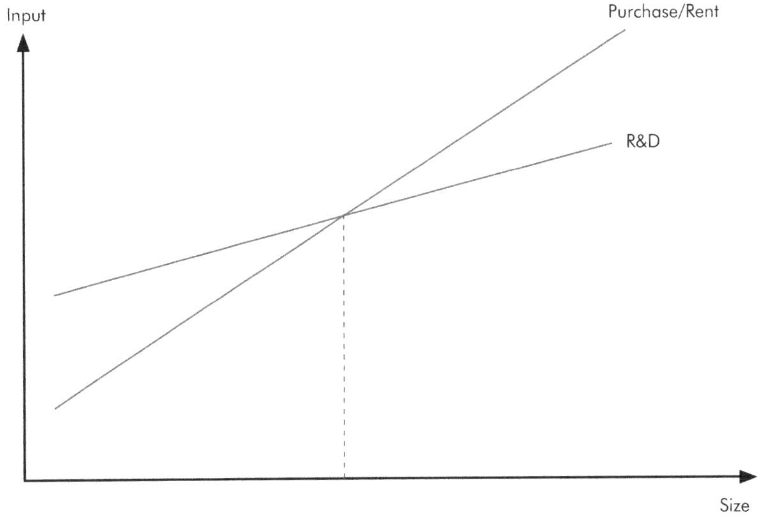

Fourth, a self-developed system could be constantly optimized in multiple tiers of software and hardware.

History always sees amazing coincidences. Just when we were about to develop a file storage system, Google went ahead of us. In 2007, they released a thesis about the design of GFS (Google File System), which gave us a lot of inspiration. Then we developed a Taobao-oriented image storage system, Taobao File System (TFS). Three years later, we found that the coincidences in history were even more miraculous than we had imagined. Almost at the same time of our development, another Chinese Internet company also developed its own file storage system—TFS, one with the same name as ours (Guess which company it was).

In June 2007, TFS was officially launched. The size of the cluster applied in the real operations reached 200 PC (146GB×6 SAS 15KB

Raid5); the number of files reached hundreds of millions; the storage capacity of system deployment was 140TB; the storage capacity in actual use was 50TB; one server supported random IOPS 200+, running at 3MB/s.

To describe the system architecture of TFS, we have to explain the business demands first. Taobao's demands for image storage can be roughly described as follows:

Files are small with high concurrency; more reading operations are needed than writing ones; visits are random; no modifications are necessary; storage costs should be low; the system should be disaster tolerant and provide backup. Obviously, to meet these demands, we should adopt a distributed storage system; as the files have unified sizes, we can use a proprietary file system; the high concurrency and random reading and writing require fewer I/O operations; considering costs and backup, we need cheap storage facilities; disaster recovery requires smooth capacity expansion.

We developed TFS 1.0 based on GFS after optimizing GFS substantially. The following is the architecture chart of TFS 1.0.

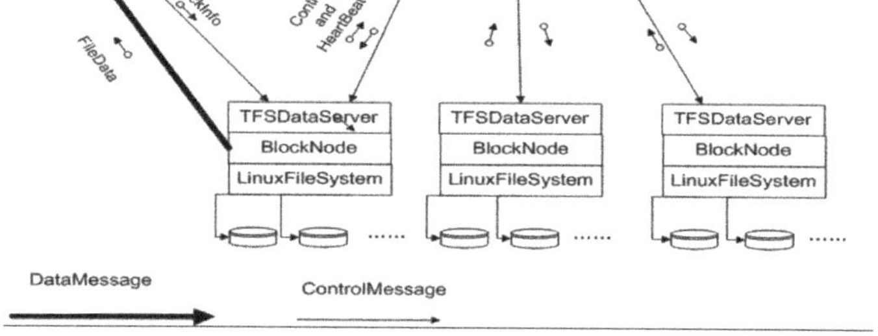

As you can see from the above architecture chart, the cluster is composed of a pair of Name Servers and several Data Servers. The two Name Servers form a computer duplex. And that is the concept of supervisor node in a clustered file system.

In this system:

- each Data Server runs on a common Linux host;
- data files are stored in the form of Blocks (a Block is usually 64MB);
- the storage of multiple Blocks is to guarantee data security;
- ext3 file system is adopted to store data files;
- raid5 is used to deal with redundant data;
- file names have built-in metadata information, the connection between user-saved TFS file names and the actual file names, which made the amount of metadata rather small.

TFS's biggest trick in its core design lies in the treatment of metadata. There is only one copy of metadata in a conventional clustered system and it's managed by a supervisor node, which tends to cause a bottleneck. As Taobao's users don't care about under what names the images are saved, TFS builds some metadata information in the names of the image files, such as the size of an image, time, and visit frequency, including its logical block number, but the actual metadata contain little information. Therefore the structure of metadata is very simple. Merely one FileID can tell you the exact position of a file. As a mass of file information is hidden in the file names, the whole system completely abandons the conventional structure of a directory tree, which demands a tremendous cost. As the directory tree is removed, the scalability of the entire cluster can be improved greatly. In fact, this design concept is similar to the "object-based storage" currently popular in the industry.

Before TFS was launched, Taobao only allowed the uploading of one picture for each commodity and the image size should have been less than 120KB; the pictures in the item description had to use the services of an external website. It was indeed troublesome to release an item back then. I once intended to sell a second-hand computer and uploaded the pictures onto a Google album first. After the item was released in Taobao, I found my Google album was blocked and my uploaded pictures couldn't be seen. I was very upset then. After the launch of TFS, the number of item demonstration pictures was expanded to five and also the picture services provided by Taobao became available to the pictures in item description. At present, Taobao offers 1GB of space for each user's pictures. In this way, technology and business are boosted by supplementation. When business requirements can't be met, technology must be innovated. And after technology is innovated, there will be a larger scope of development for business.

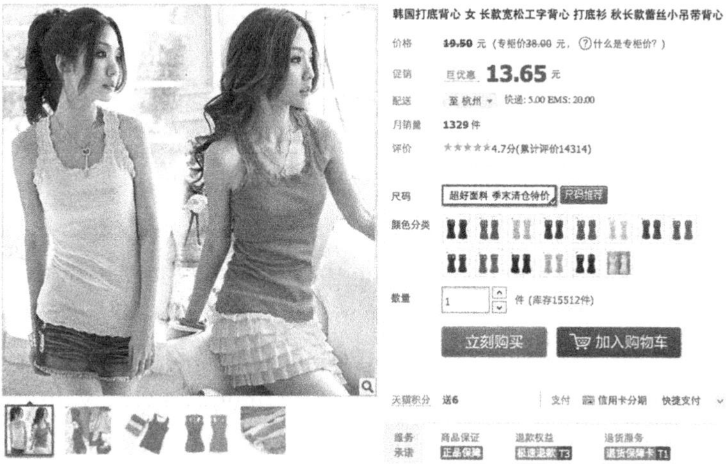

After it was released, TFS went through multiple modifications based on different versions. By the time version 1.3 was released in June, 2009, it had already become a rather mature system, and the cluster size had been expanded greatly. It was deployed on Taobao's image operation system. The whole system had been enlarged from the original 200 PC Servers to 440 PC Servers (300B×12 SAS 15KB RPM) plus 30 PC Servers (600B×12 SAS 15KB RPM). The number of files being supported was also expanded to the tens of billions; the storage capacity for system deployment was 1,800TB; the actual storage capacity was 995TB; one Data Server supported random IOPS900+, running at 15MB+; and the physical memory for the running of Name Server was 217MB (with a 1,000M network card for the server).

The network topology of TFS version 1.3 is shown in the picture below.

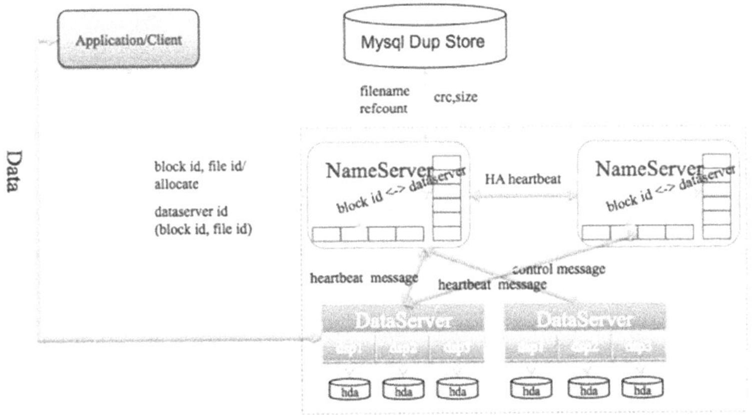

With TFS version 1.3, engineers focused on improving the performance of heartbeat and synchronization. In the new version, heartbeat and synchronization could be switched in only a few seconds; and some optimizations were made, including the storage of metadata in memory and the clearing of disk space. Improvements were also made in performance in the following aspects:

- the ext4 file system was adopted and files were pre-allocated to reduce the performance loss caused by the data fragments of the ex3 file system and others;
- one single disk was managed by one process and RAID5 was eliminated;
- the central control node attached with HA mechanism achieved balance between stability and performance complexity;
- the size of metadata was reduced and more metadata was loaded into memory to improve the access speed;
- load balancing of the crossing assembly rack and IDC and redundancy security policy;
- completely smooth capacity expansion.

For picture services as a whole, the use of TFS is far from enough. The topology structure of all the image servers is shown in the picture below.

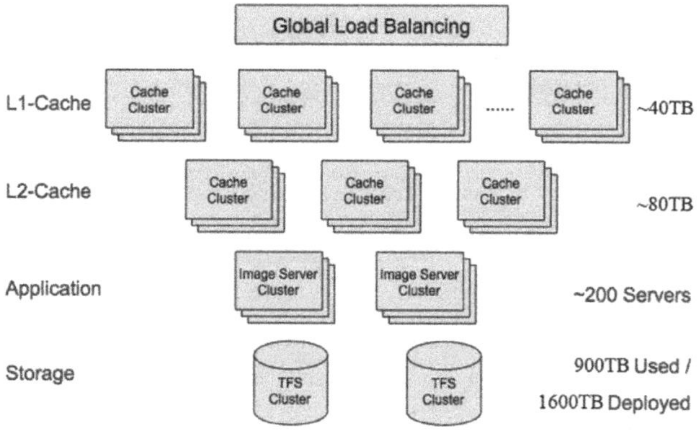

The entire image storage system is like a huge server with processing, cache, and storage units. We have described the back-end TFS clustered file storage system, and at the front-end of TFS, more than 200 image file servers are deployed via Apache for the calculations in generating thumbnails.

One particular thing is that Taobao's thumbnails are generated in real time according to Taobao's rules about thumbnail generation. This has two advantages: First of all, it can avoid too many image files being stored in the back-end image servers and substantially save the back-end storage space. Our calculations show that the way of generating real-time thumbnails can save 90% of storage space compared with the mode of generating all thumbnails in advance. That is to say, in the first way, the storage space cost is only 10% as much as that of the second one. Second, thumbnails can be generated in real time according to requirements. This is a more flexible way.

The front end of the image file servers has L1-cache and L2-cache with a global load balancer in the front end to address the hotspots pictures. There must be some images hot spots. The thing is, it's best to make the images hit in the cache as much as possible. Taobao has established L2-cache in the central points of the carriers and L1-cache in the central point of the entire system. Together with the global load balancer, they keep the traffic delivered to the back-end TFS well balanced and divided and greatly improve the response performance of the front end. According to Taobao's cache strategies, we try to make most of the images hit in the cache. If it can't be achieved, a query will be sent to the local servers to search for the original image and generate a thumbnail accordingly. If an image can't be hit in either way, it'll be retrieved from the back-end TFS clustered file storage system. Therefore, the traffic that's finally delivered to TFS clustered file storage system is greatly optimized.

Taobao programs image processing and cache into a Nginx-based module. We believe that Nginx is an HTTP server with the best performance to date as it has clear codes and great modularity. Taobao uses Graphics Magick to process images and employs the cache file system targeting small objects. At the front end LVS+Haproxy deploys the queries for the original image and all of its thumbnails to the same Image Server.

Regarding file positioning, the Hash algorithm is used for the indexing of memory and the discs have to be read once at most. In addition, there will be a lot of identical images being uploaded repeatedly, and the duplicated files will be removed with Hash algorithm too. Disc writing is achieved via the Append procedure and the elimination strategy FIFO is adopted. We try to reduce writing operations on the discs instead of further increasing the hit ratio of Cache. As Image Server and TFS are located in the same data center, the disc reading efficiency is very high.

Currently Taobao's TFS is open source (see code.taobao.org). Experts in this industry can use the system and work together to perfect it.

Taobao KV Cache System — Tair

The development of TFS has brought to full play the image functions of Taobao. Just like TFS, many other technologies have been developed under the requirements of products. Before introducing the following technology, I'll first talk about a few products we developed a few years ago.

Let's see a tragic one first: group buying, which was different from the Groupon-style program we see everywhere nowadays. In 2006, before Groupon was born, Taobao's Product Manager Yideng had already proposed the idea of "group buying." According to Yideng's initial vision, one buyer initiated a group buying attempt in the community and when the group leader had collected enough people they went to bargain with the seller. It's comparable to the "free group" of the current Mogujie (a Chinese online shopping website). However, due to various reasons, some functions of the product were cut off during the development process, which made the product veer off the original course a bit. In the actual version, a seller set the group buying price and the deal was made when buyers reached a certain number. This function appeared to be a transaction mode combining Taobao's "Fixed Price" and "Dutch Auction" programs, but it didn't last too long. The most noticeable weakness of this transaction mode was that it allowed buyers to know a sellers' bottom line. Even if not enough buyers came together to start a group buy, they would try to bargain with the seller at the group buying price. Back then, to increase the number of page views, Taobao opened a group buying zone. Honest sellers suffered from losses in bargains—as there were not enough buyers for group buying—while crafty ones jacked up product prices and drew on the group buying zone for promotion. In the following two years, this product was reduced to a promotion tool. (To be honest, the group buying offers we currently see everywhere are actually promotions too.) This product gave the R&D staff a deep understanding of the concept of "product."

And there's a more tragic product, namely "My Taobao." This is where Taobao's members manage their products, transactions, delivery addresses, comments, and complaints. As this section can only be seen after a member logs in, it used to have a completely different style and interface, and was not optimized for a long time. The interface looked unpleasant and it was also inconvenient for users to use. If a seller had lots of products, he would have to deal with them one by one when he wanted to release them or remove them off the shelves. That was really troublesome (just think about those book sellers). At that time, an important figure came and that was Chengzhi, current CEO of Mogujie. He demonstrated to us the most advanced front-end interaction technique, just like the interactive AJAX of Gmail. You can drag, use the right mouse button, or employ composite keys. And you needn't refresh the page when an operation

is completed. It's an amazing technology for product management. It's really cool! I was Project Manager of the project and Yideng was Product Manager. Together with Wanjian and some other engineers, we began and kept working enthusiastically for three months. When we were about to finish, Mr. Ma suddenly appeared behind me. After he watched me operate the new version of "My Taobao," he asked me whether it was a kind of client-end software, but I told him it was a web page. He couldn't believe it, saying it was the same as a client-end software, for it did not have an underline beneath a link and used file folders for the release and removal of products. He said even he didn't know how to operate it, let alone the sellers.

Look at the ingenious page-turning bar, the exquisite file folder structure, the humanized check boxes, and an Excel-like window-freezing function. How sexy it is!

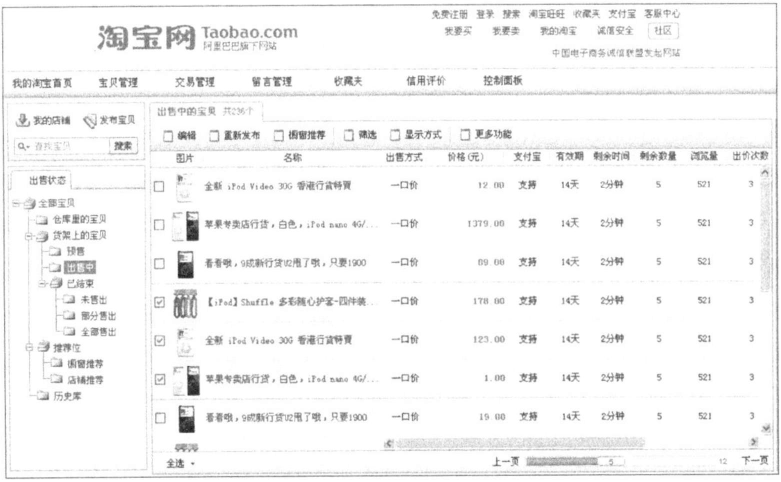

Mr. Ma is indeed a genius. His prediction justified itself. The first mass disturbance in Taobao's history broke out. After sellers tried the new version of "My Taobao," many of them went mad, saying they didn't know how to operate it. Yideng and Chengzhi worked together trying to modify the page into one that was closer to a web page. After half a month's modifications, though, the sellers' anger still remained. Seeing the two of them hanging there, I was frustrated and talked with the supervisors for a solution. Then we put up a vote on the forum about whether the new version of "My Taobao" should be used and the result showed over a half of the voters opposed it. So, the system that cost a dozen people's three-month work was killed. I was very upset about it, but what troubled us the most was that after the new version was halted, some other sellers got angry saying how come such a great function was canceled. From this experience we learn that we must be very prudent when trying new technologies (AJAX and prototype framework) or changing users' regular operation habits. However, one lesson we failed to learn was that we were at a loss when dealing with a mass disturbance. In the later mass disturbances caused by "Wealth Pull" and Taobao Mall, I found the previous tragedy repeated.

Speaking of "Wealth Pull," it's actually the most tragic product. On the May Day of 2006, an epoch-making project was launched. "God of Wealth" said the project would include the best employees and I was selected. That I was classified into the category of the best employees eased my pain from the brutality of "My Taobao." It was a system of P4P products. With this system, sellers paid according to the deals. We thought many sellers had made a fortune and they would be willing to pay for their products to be listed in the front rows, since there were so many products on Taobao and it was very difficult to locate one. We allowed sellers to buy advertisement spaces and ranked their products based on a certain algorithm (similar to Baidu's rank bidding). The ranks depended on the sellers' credit, transaction volume, as well as how many times the products had been collected and how much the sellers paid. That was an extremely complex algorithm. What a wonderful profit-earning pattern it could be!

This system went on smoothly, but when it was released, a more serious mass disturbance broke out. The sellers questioned, "Haven't you promised that you won't charge any fees in three years? Doesn't the advertising cost count?" Then our competitors fueled the disturbance, making a stir in various social networks, and one competing company even put forward the function of "one click to move" to receive our members. All of a sudden, the public got angry and everyone blamed us. To pacify the angry sellers, we once again put up a vote in the forum and let our users decide whether the function should be canceled. And it came to a tragic end, the same as "My Taobao." And just like what happened with "My Taobao," after "Wealth Pull" was canceled, some sellers who enjoyed the function questioned the decision. (After Yahoo China was merged into Alibaba, a similar function — "Taobao Express" — was developed, and thus met the requirements of these sellers.)

Although "Wealth Pull" proved to be a failure, this project had made deeper technological explorations including the technique of following user behaviors and AJAX. One of the techniques is very classic. On Taobao's website, the item description pages have hundreds of millions of page views every day and all the pages are stored in the cache. In the function of "Wealth Pull" we showed the sellers how many times their items had been browsed (see the following picture), and the figures must be updated in real time. But cache is usually updated asynchronously. Therefore, at first we never thought of putting those figures in the cache. We increased a field in the item tables. Whenever a new PV was created, this field was updated. Then, one hour after the function was launched, the database broke down, as it couldn't bear it. Common cache strategies don't support real-time updates. Then our genius Duolong came up with an idea: write a module in Apache. The figures are written into a collected cache zone in Apache without accessing the lower WebApp container. Then the data in the cache zone is updated into the database asynchronously. As I said before: all the item description pages are stored in the cache. The cache is used to the extreme.

Next, let's talk about the technology of cache.

Taobao began to adopt cache technology long ago. In 2004, we employed a cache called ESI (Edge Side Includes). Before we employed ESI, Duolong tried many Java caches, but they were all quite heavy. Then we used Oracle Web Cache, which often broke down too. As Oracle Web Cache also supported ESI, Duolong discovered the wonderful ESI. ESI is a data buffering/caching server. It provides the technologies and services of buffering/caching Web pages (page fragments). Previous data buffering servers worked with pages. The pages were copied into the data buffering servers. This method is very effective in dealing with static pages, but with dynamic pages, it is inefficient. ESI buffers part of the Web pages. XML marks help specify the parts to be buffered. As a result, a Web page is divided into the dynamic changing part and the static unchanged part, and only the static part is delivered to the server. Although most of Taobao's data is dynamic, there are still lots of static fragments on the Web pages, such as the head and bottom of a page, the seller's information on the item description page (see the right side of the following picture). All of them were retrieved from the ESI cache at the beginning.

Since ESI is able to help with the caching of the static fragments of Web pages, clever readers may wonder: can the back-end data be cached too? Of course they can, and must be. For example, a big seller's items and shop may have millions of page views every day while a small seller only a few. If the big seller's user information has to be retrieved from the database each time, it will definitely be inefficient. But if the information is stored in the memory and retrieved from the memory, it will perform well. This is where the Key-value oriented memcached system comes in. Unfortunately, when Taobao was in dire need of memcached, it hadn't been created (it came into existence in June 2003 but didn't become popular until recent years.) Our genius architect Duolong once again displayed his talent. He wrote a cache system called TBstore which is a distributed cache system based on the Berkeley DB. After the system was released, it was widely used inside Alibaba Group, Taobao in particular. TBstore contained ESI, Checkcode, Description, Story (a long field in the item information, whose length is second only to item description), and user information.

TBstore's operation process: The Hash function is used according to the saved search key, and a Hash value is returned. Then a modulo operation is done with the Hash value and the figure in the general cache server. Next, the cache server marked with the remainder of the modulo operation in the server list is found. Finally, Java Client API does the encapsulation. There needs to be no concern about application.

TBstore has an advantage: As its storage is based on Berkeley DB, which will write data on disks when data amount exceeds memory capacity, the storage is sustainable. But this is TBstore's disadvantage too. Once data are written into disks, the caching performance will be sharply weakened.

At that time, another project spurred Taobao's improvement in the cache technology. In 2007, we singled out Taobao's user information and built a UIC (User Information Center). As all of Taobao's functions depend on user information, they all have to be singled out. Otherwise systems to follow would have problems in expansion. When an application system visits UIC, it accesses the database for user information. Roughly speaking, several billion items of user information need to be retrieved every day. If the database had to respond to all of the requests, it would certainly break down. As a result, a cache system must be applied. Duolong specially developed a cache system for UIC and called it TDBM, which abandoned the sustainable storage function of Berkeley DB and stores all data in the memory. In 2009, Duolong improved TDBM's clustered distribution mode based on the memory structure of memchached. Then TDBM 2.0 was released, which greatly increased memory utilization and throughput.

The picture below shows the monitored real-time information of a critical application. The first row stands for the hit ratio of UIC's cache. As we can see, the hit ratio is as high as 99.2%. In other words, 99.2% of the pressure is reduced from the database.

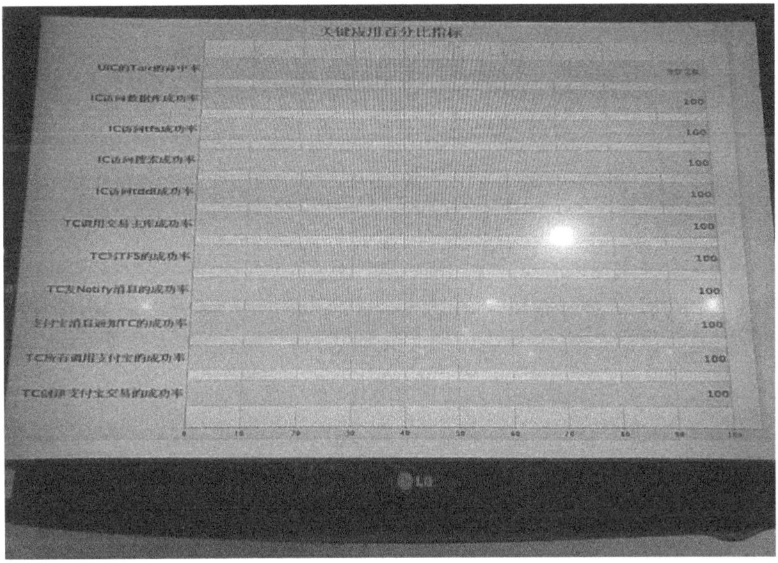

As the data interfaces and usages of TDBM and TBstore are similar, the development team combined the two and released the self-developed Key-Value cache system — Tair (Taobao Pair, where

Pair means Key-Value data pairs). Tair has two storage functions: cache and sustainable storage. As a distributed system, Tair consists of a central control node and a series of service nodes. We call the former Config Server and the latter Data Server. Config Server controls all the Data Servers, monitoring all the Data Server's conditions. Data Server provides all kinds of data services, and reports their own conditions to the Config Server in the form of heartbeat. Config Server is the control point and a single point. Currently we have a main Config Server and a backup one to ensure its reliability. All of the Data Servers have equal status. Tair's structure is shown in the picture below.

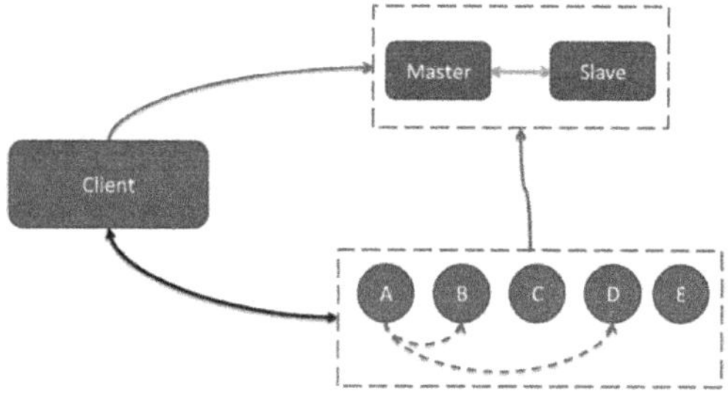

The system's deployment structure is shown in the picture below.

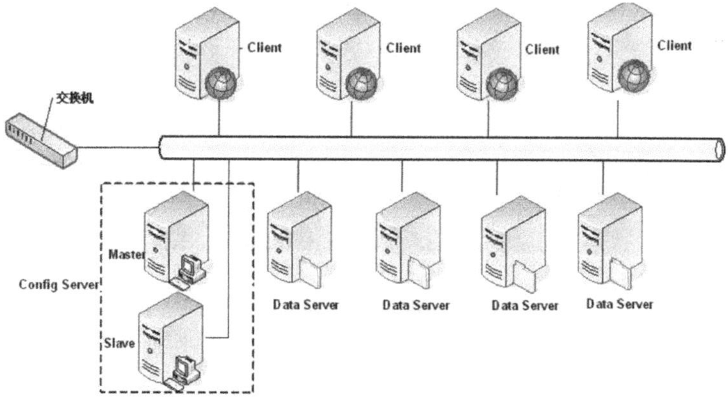

For the time being, Tair provides support for the cache information of nearly all Taobao systems. Tair is open source now. Its address is code.taobao.org.

After the creation of TFS and Tair, the structure of the entire system is shown in the picture below.

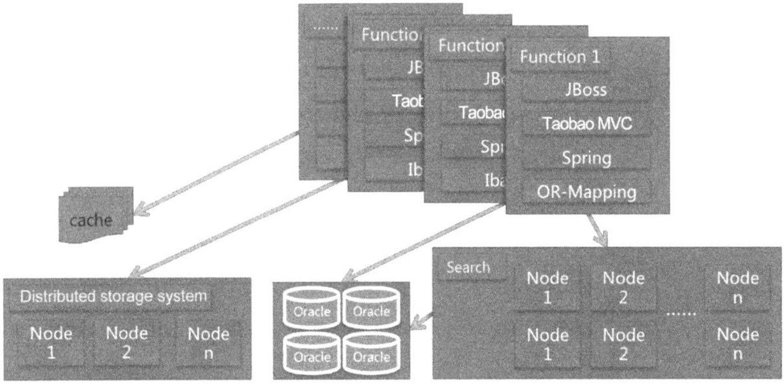

At this time, the R&D department upgraded the search engine iSearch too. Previously the search engine dispatched data to multiple machines, and no item of information had any copy. Now every item has several copies. The entire system is changed into a matrix from a single-line deployment. It can support larger visiting volumes and has higher usability.

By 2007, Taobao had had an average of 250 million PVs every day, more than 100 million commodities, over 50 million registered members, and a gross merchandise volume of RMB 43.3 billion across the site.

CHAPTER 5

Distributed E-Commerce Operating System

Behind the facade of a rapid development were some hidden hazards. Restricted by the technical architecture, it was more difficult to perform teamwork. In addition, the code was getting more bloated and the development efficiency was diminishing; with an increasing demand for new services, the system was swamped with old business. How to adjust the architecture in this situation? Then there came a radical change to the system and the distributed e-commerce operating system came into existence. With the help of the system, we were emboldened to conduct the "Double 11" online shopping campaign annually.

- **Servitization**
- **Middleware**
- **The Session Framework**
- **Taobao Open Platform**

The vision of the architects is essential in the process of system development. Being a programmer, you only need to consider how to get the code to function, while being an architect, you have to consider the scalability and reusability of the system. Someone called such acute sense of scalability and reusability as "code mysophobia." During the early days of Taobao, there were several architects who had this kind of sense. Zhou Yuehong developed Webx which was a framework with strong scalability, and Xingdian inserted modules of database sharding and routing as well as a Session to the framework. These modules were required when developing the background system of Taobao, and Xingdian gave me instructions on how to package these modules into JAR packages separately. In addition, when we were developing the Taobao Plane Ticket System and the Taobao Lottery System, there were a lot of things on pages that required reuse, among which headers and footers were the most obvious examples. At the beginning, each system copied the same headers and footers, but there was a time when we had to change the footers frequently. For example, we at first changed "Yahoo China" to "China Yahoo." However, after Koubei was integrated with China Yahoo, the footers became "Yahoo Koubei", and finally became "China Yahoo" again. Later, I separated the Velocity template of this part from the others, making it a common module.

Servitization

The above mentioned modules were small reused ones. In 2006, we reformed product categories, introducing in the concept of property. This project was named "Mount Tai" (one of the 5 sacred mountains in China, located in Shandong Province), which implied its significance: it would become an epoch-making innovation. In the preceding three years before the launching of the project, the classification of products was shown in tree structures. As the number of products increased, their categories became more and more detailed and complex; and consequently, buyers had to figure out which class a product belonged to before they searched for it and opened the categories in a step-down approach. Employees of Taobao's operations department that took charge of the categories also found a serious problem. For example, men's clothing was classified into T-shirt, Nike T-shirt, Nike T-shirt made of cotton in a step-down order, and so was women's clothing. It was confusing that whether to first classify the clothing into men's clothing and women's clothing, and then further classify the two kinds of clothing by style, brand, and material; or to classify the clothing by brand first, and then by style, material, and the person it was designed for. It was at this point that Yideng entered the scene, saying that brand, style and material could be collectively referred to as the "properties" of a product. The "property" was a new concept which was similar to Tag, but it was more discrete and flexible, and reduced tiers of categories. This concept solved the problem of classification at one stroke. From the perspective of the system, we established a data structure for "property", and because of the fact that not only the sub-nodes of categories had properties, but also the parent nodes as well. Hence the combination of the categories and the properties could still be a structured data object. After such a system was established, we made it a separate service, naming it Catserver (Category Server). We also separated the search function which was closely related to the categories and properties of products and named it Hesper. Both Catserver and Hesper could be used by Taobao's foreground and background systems.

At present, Taobao boasts the largest number of categories and properties of products in the world. One can find almost all kinds of products on Taobao (except those prohibited). However, after the initial improvement of categories and properties of products, we were in property data, especially those of digital products. To solve this problem, we cooperated with "Zhongguancun Online" and obtained a lot of data. At that time, properties of many products were labeled as "from Zhongguancun Online." This data facilitated our operation. In consideration of the fact that the operation of Taobao was primarily based upon the operation of categories, we had to provide different products according to different seasons. This meant that an adjustment needed to be made on the categories and properties of products so that buyers could find what they needed more easily. For example, in summer, we asked users to highlight the material of women's clothing listed in the first category, indicating whether it is made of lace or 100% cotton, while in winter, we would ask them to list down coats under the first category. Products in vogue should be put under higher categories. The frequent adjustments of categories and properties led to a problem: as sellers were required to edit the information of their products whenever there was an adjustment of categories, their workload grew along with the increasing number of products, which would consequently wear them out. In 2008, we conducted research in the classification of products in the sales areas and the warehouse areas of supermarkets. We found that products in sales areas were arranged according to season or products' linkage between each other (for instance, the famous beer and diapers story) whereas products in the warehouses were stored according to their natural categories. The two were closely related, yet separated from each other. Sellers released products according to their natural categories and properties while for foreground operation of Taobao, products were displayed in a way their categories and properties were according to the operational needs. The improved service of categories and properties of products was named Forest (Forest was very much like the departments and properties of commodities, and Catserver was also used to offer services concerning branding, key words, and the authorization of sellers). The servitization of categories and properties was Taobao's first exploration of the servitization of its system.

Although some architects had code mysophobia, yet the workload and the code volume increased explosively. Service receivers were always urging developers to work more quickly. Given the heavy workload, new developers were recruited. These new developers knew nothing about the former operations, so they had no choice but to add some "proper code" to some "proper places." The added code might seem to work well and was then released. Thereupon, a vicious circle was formed, in which the whole system became unwieldy, the coupling of different businesses increased, and the development productivity of code decreased. There was a popular saying at that time that "half an hour would have passed after you wrote a piece of code and had it accepted after compiling; and half a day would have passed if the code was rejected after compiling." In that case, the system was more likely to be at fault. It was often the case that a transaction would go wrong after you changed certain code related to the products. Moreover, there would be something wrong with AliWangWang if you changed some certain code of the BBS of Taobao. The developers were plagued with the problem while the service receivers thought that the developers were slack in their work.

By the end of 2007, Lu Peng, a senior executive from the Silicon Valley who was nicknamed Master Kongwen (a master of martial arts in Chinese wuxia novels) came to the R&D Department of Taobao. He was a gentle and kind, and told us that everything should be centered on maintaining stability and every factor that caused instability should be eliminated. For example, whenever we made a daily modification, we must conduct regression testing of the whole system. Otherwise, when we have several modifications made in the same version, the whole system should not be released if one modification of the function failed in the testing. We called it the "train mode," which meant that the train would not depart until all passengers were aboard. The adoption of this mode led directly to the delay of the train which meant that the release of a new function was delayed. It was easy to see the discontent of the users and Kongwen was definitely under great pressure.

In retrospect, we didn't really understand his train of thought. Subject to the above-mentioned requirements, we had to make some changes. For example, we must conduct regression testing every day, running through the whole system every night. In addition, we had to decompose and reconstruct this highly complicated system. We separated the module with the highest reusability from the others, naming it UIC (User Information Center). UIC only dealt with the operation of the most basic user information, such as Gettysburg and getUserByName.

There were another two new services that required splitting of the system's basic functions. We were developing two new services then, Taobao Trip (trip.taobao.com) and Taobao Lottery (caipiao.taobao.com), both of which differed from the services on the master station in terms of product display and the transaction process. Plane tickets were demonstrated according to their flight information, and lottery according to Union Lotto, numbers, and the schedule for football matches. Yet both used almost the same member and transaction management functions as the master station. The problem was that, if we operated the two new services on the master station, there would be a lot of things irrelevant to the services on the master station; but if we established a new station for new services, there would be much duplication. At last, we decided not to mess up the master station and established two new service systems instead. We wrote a new set of codes for the entire process of services offered, including searching for products, buying products, evaluation and feedback, and checking orders. Today, if you check the transaction record in "My Taobao," you will find that plane tickets and lottery are listed independently in "what I bought" instead of being listed with other orders. At that time, if we separated modules concerning members, transactions, products, and comments from the others, we would not have needed to write the code all over again.

It can be seen from the navigation bar on the left side of "My Taobao" that orders of plane tickets, lottery, and online games are listed separately.

By early 2008, the whole master station had almost met its maximum capacity with more than 100 million product listings, over 250 million PVs and more than 50 million registered users. There was a shortage of connection pools of Oracle and the database also reached its capacity limit. Even if we added machines to the upper-level system, the database could not be expanded. Therefore, we had to further break up basic services and start expansion from the low-level system so that the upper-level one might be expanded. In this way we would be able to accommodate the increasing services in the next three to five years.

We also launched a larger project in which we separated transaction, our core service module, from others. The original version of transaction on Taobao was coupled with both product management and Alipay, which led to a complex system and poor user experiences. We singled out the low-level transaction service, naming it the Trade Center (TC). The so-called low-level services were actually about atomic operations like creating orders, reducing inventories and changing the status of orders. The upper-level transaction service was called Trade Manager (TM). For example, when a physical product was sold, operations needed to be conducted with the orders, inventories, and logistics; when it comes to a virtual product, there was no need to deal with the logistics, and all could be done with the TM. This project got an unimaginative name.

"Qingdao Lake." which embodied the developers' longing for a trip to the place, and their hope was fulfilled later. At that time, we were engaged in developing the Taobao Mall. The aforesaid basic services that were separated laid a good foundation for the rapid establishment of the Taobao Mall.

We gained a lot of experience in system architecture during the process of splitting such modules as categories and properties, the user center, and the transaction center, as well as during the process of servitization. At the end of 2008, we launched a larger project: modularizing all services of Taobao. This was the second radical change we had made after 2004, when we moved from the LAMP architecture to the Java architecture. We gave the project a really cool name, "Hashish" (literally meaning the color cobblestone which was used to patch up the sky in an ancient Chinese creation myth.) The reconstruction of the system was just like an adventure, and someone compared it to changing the engine of a speeding plane. After the project was launched, all the participating engineers made a trip to Sanya on the island paradise of Hainan Province to enjoy themselves for several days.

The beautiful scenery of Sanya is obviously much better than that of the Qiandao Lake. I have visited the Qiandao Lake for at least five times since I came to Taobao. Every time in cerebration of a new project, there will always be some new colleagues clamoring for "a trip to the Qiandao Lake," though I think that they need higher pursuits.

They split the Taobao system into the architecture below:

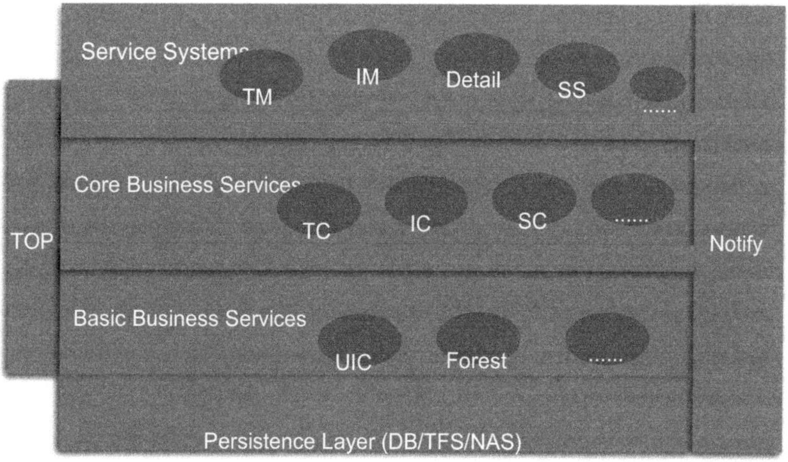

UIC and Forest have already been mentioned in the preceding part of the chapter. TC, IC and SC respectively refer to Trade Center, Item Center and Shop Center. These central services provided only atomic service logic, being in charge of such operations as searching for products according to ID, creating transactions and reducing inventories. Service systems that had a higher level included TM (Trade Manager), IM (Item Manager), SM (Shop Manager, which was renamed as SS later, referring to Shop System), and Detail (product details).

After the breakup, the interactive relationships between systems became very complex, for which a diagram is shown in Picture 1.

The benefits for breaking up the system like this were pretty obvious: first, different systems could be operated separately after the breakup with each system managing just simple services, which made it easier for the databases to be expanded; second, there were a lot of reusable modules, which made it easier to develop new services; and third, we could have each service operated by specially-assigned persons so that every technician could concentrate more on one particular area. The issues required to be solved were also self-evident. First, the systems still had connections with each other after the breakup, and those at lower levels were more likely to be used by customers, which required super-large capacity and high availability of the low-level systems. In addition, there was a problem as to how to achieve communication between systems after the breakup. We needed two pieces of middleware to achieve communication. One was the real-time middle ware (HSF, high-speed service framework) and the other was the asynchronous message-oriented middleware (Notify). Another issue to be solved was how to save users' login information when they transferred to system B after having logged on

Picture 1

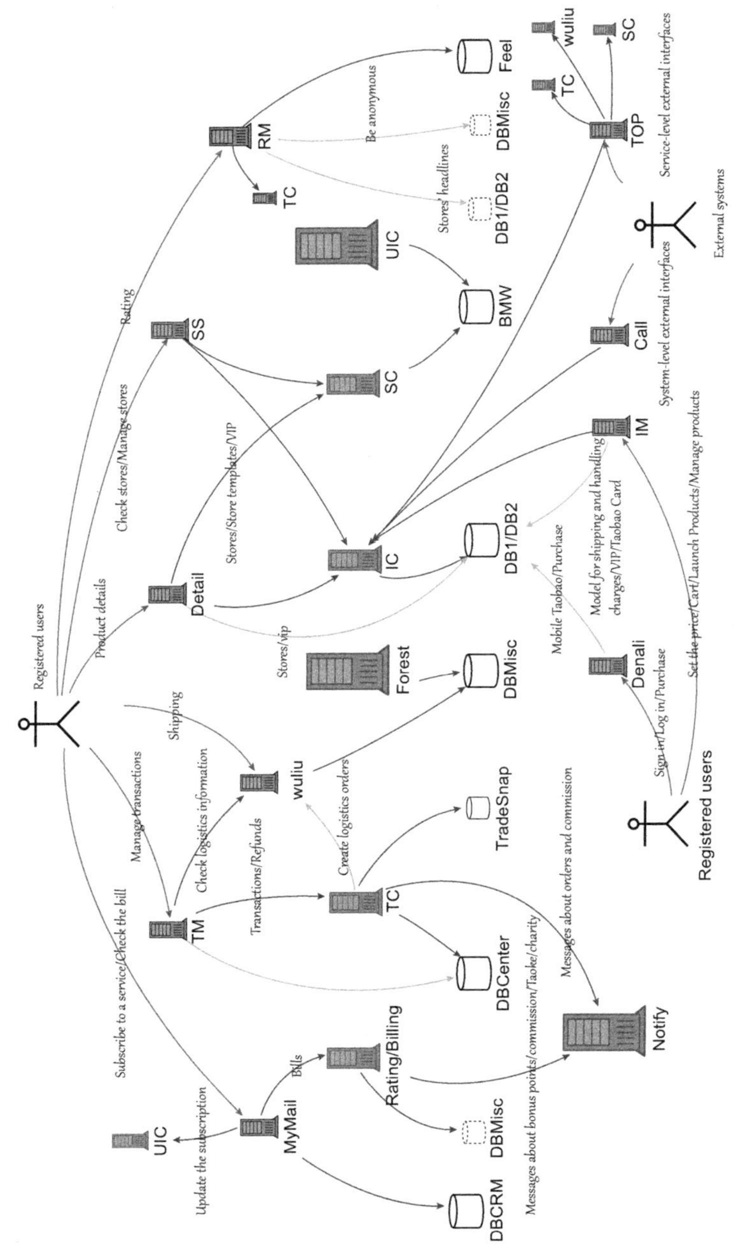
Registered users
Rating
Check stores/Manage stores
Product details
Shipping
Manage transactions
Check logistics information
Subscribe to a service/Check the bill
Update the subscription
Bills
Transactions/Refunds
Create logistics orders
Stores/Store templates/VIP
Stores/vip
Be anonymous
Stores' headlines
Messages about orders and commission
Messages about bonus points/commission/Taoke/charity
Mobile Taobao/Purchase
Model for shipping and handling charges/VIP/Taobao Card
Set the price/Cart/Launch Products/Manage products
Sign in/Log in/Purchase
System-level external interfaces
Service-level external interfaces
External systems
RM
TC
Feel
DBMisc
DB1/DB2
TOP
wuliu
SC
UIC
BMW
SS
Call
IM
IC
Detail
Forest
Denali
TradeSnap
TM
DBCenter
Notify
Rating/Billing
MyMail
DBCRM

system A, the process of which involved a Session framework. Finally there was an issue concerning software engineering—how shall we test such a multi-level system?

Middleware

The development of the Internet system seems rather professional. However, in fact, there are similar "systems" in our daily life. Just as a philosopher once said, "there is nothing new under the sun." We may learn the development of a website system through an example of our life. This example was illustrated by Bixuan, creator of HSF.

A cashier in a small supermarket may do some extra work, such as cleaning and arranging the product displays.

As the number of customers increases, there are usually long queues in front of the checkout, which may be unbearable to the other customers. Therefore, another checkout is added and a new cashier is employed.

The cashiers would have no time to do the cleaning when there are dozens of customers. Soon the supermarket gets a bit dirty and another person is duly employed for the cleaning.

As the number of customers continually increases, the supermarket goes through several renovations from the original one-story structure into a two-story one. Then more checkouts are being added, and more cashiers and cleaners being employed.

In the operation process of the supermarket, the boss finds that there are long queues in front of some of the checkouts while for the others things are just the other way round. Probing into the reasons, he realizes that with too many checkouts up there, customers cannot see the guest flow before them all. One simple solution to this is to add more checkouts. However, there is no more room for new checkouts and furthermore, the boss doesn't want to hire too many employees. So he adopts another solution which is to install a camera and a large screen from which customers can see the traffic flow of every checkout. In this way, the problem is basically solved.

After queues in front of all checkouts have been almost of the same length, a new problem arises. The queues before some of the checkouts move much more slowly than those before the others as a result of the fact that some customers have put into their shopping cart a particularly large number of things. A new solution is proposed, which is about setting up special checkouts for customers who buy less than 10 pieces of products so that these people don't have to wait in long queues. After the proposal is adopted, there comes a noticeable increase in customer satisfaction and also a growth in sales. Similar solutions are used to deal with problems concerning group buying and VIPs.

Having resolved the aforesaid vexations, the boss notices another long-standing phenomenon that cashiers are much busier in the evening than the daytime. To save money,, he decides to have some cashiers work only in the evening and close some of the checkouts during the daytime. Customers are informed of the closed checkouts through the large screen, which prevents them from going to such checkouts. The cost is thus greatly cut down.

This daily-life example and its solutions are comparable to the case of some technologies applied in the development of websites. The only difference is that the example and solutions have new names in the technical sense, such as cluster, work division, load balancing and QoS–based resource allocation.

- Cluster: All cashiers provide the same function for customers. No matter which checkout a customer goes to, he/she can complete the payment. It can be considered that these cashiers have formed a cluster where they work based on one rationale that when the number of customers increases, more cashiers are needed. In real life, however, the employment of more cashiers is restricted by space. As to Internet applications, whether these applications can form a cluster depends on the horizontal scalability of the applications, and the size of the cluster is subject to dispatch, the database, and the computer room.

- Work division: It is easy to separate the work of a cashier from that of a cleaner, but the division of work on the Internet requires important and complicated technologies, and is more difficult to achieve than that in the real life. Such a division of work mainly involves the breakup of the system according to different functions and databases. It faces two challenges: one is how to split the system and the other is how to achieve interactions between different parts after the breakup. Therefore some basic products are created, including the high-speed communication framework, the SOA platform, massage-oriented middleware and the distributed data layer.

- Load balancing: Practices like evening up the length of queues in front of all checkouts, setting up special access for customers with fewer things to buy, group buying, and VIPs can be seen as load balancing issues brought about by the cluster. From a technical perspective, it is much more complicated a feat to achieve than in real life.

- QoS-based resource allocation: It is easy to have some of the employees work only during nighttime in real life, but it is complicated and challenging for Internet applications to do similarly.

In reference to the aforesaid real-life example, it is not difficult to come up with such solutions in the case of an increasing number of users, yet it is a complicated task to master technologies related to the above four aspects. The technologies include those for optimizing cache and CDN and achieving availability of operating condition monitoring, functional downgrading, resource degradation and flow control. They also include those for controlling cost through building computer rooms by ourselves and hardware assembly. In short, it is no mean feat to establish an Internet site because it requires a lot of technologies. Certainly, it is not easy to operate a supermarket as well.

HSF, the High-speed Service Framework

From the operation of a supermarket, we can abstractly draw some ideas about system design on how to acquire the services I need after the breakup. Services provided by each cluster are shown on a "screen," from which you are informed of different areas where certain services are provided whenever you need them. You don't need to care about the person who provides the services but go directly to the certain area as the "screen" tells you, and the system will find out the fastest service channel for you.

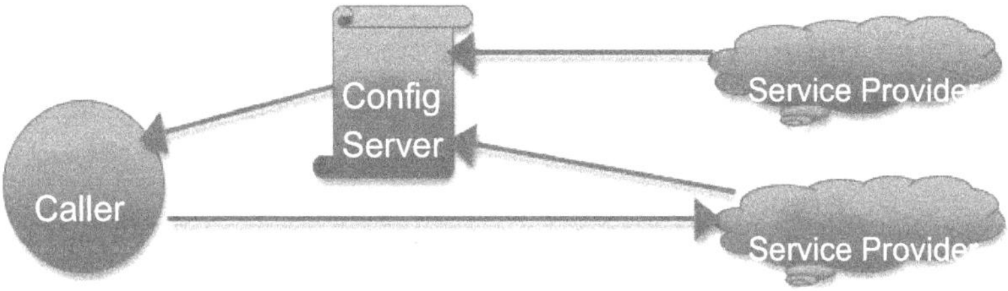

This is the rationale for design of HSF. After the startup of ConfigServer, the provider can register information (including the interface, the version, timeout, and the serialization pattern) at ConfigServer through HSF (the function of which is similar to the screen in the supermarket), whereby all services (a service may have different versions) that can be called are defined on ConfigServer. After the startup of ConfigServer, the caller can subscribe for services that he/she is interested in (including the interface and the version) at ConfigServer, and when certain information offered by the provider changes, ConfigServer will push a new service list to the caller who is interested in such services. In virtue of the service list, the caller can directly visit the corresponding service provider, without the need to use ConfigServer. We may see that ConfigServer won't push the IP address of the provider to the consumer. Instead, HSF will select a specific server according to the load status of each server and return the result to the service caller, which not only standardizes the mode for invoking services, but also achieves "soft load balancing." In normal situations, ConfigServer usually gets information on whether the provider is still in normal operation through heartbeats.

Under the support of HSF, the service cluster is "uniform" while the services are "separated" from each other to the caller. This ensures the scalability of the services and the uniformity of applications. Such scalability and uniformity, together with the "soft load balancing" provided by HSF itself, make the service layer a "private cloud" for the application layer.

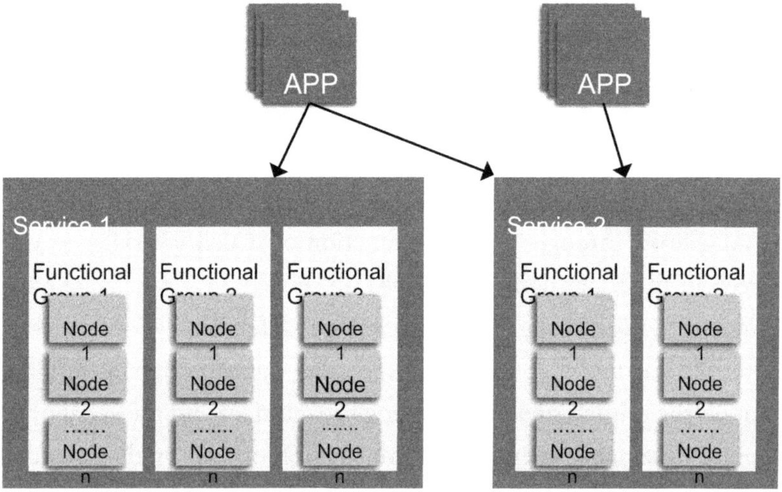

HSF is deployed under Jboss, Jetty, or Tomcat in the form of SAR packages. After an application starts up, HSF (some people in the development team call it as "Hao-ShuFu" which in Chinese literally means "so comfortable") services start, too. HSF is designed to provide a distributed service framework for applications on Taobao. It offers support to developers through distributed applications and unified ways of publishing/calling, so that they can easily develop distributed applications and provide and use public functional modules. The developers don't have to care about the various specific technologies in the distributed system, such as technologies concerning remote telecommunication, performance wastage, calling transparency, and the realization of synchronous/asynchronous calls.

The above picture implies the high speed of HSF. HSF is a distributed RPC (Remote Procedure Call Protocol) framework whose Service is defined according to OSGI, and the TCP/IP protocols are adopted at the communication layer of RPC.

It can be seen clearly from the following screenshot of HSF monitoring system that there are two servers (there are many other servers which are not cropped) in two clusters that provide the service of com.taobao.item.service.SpuGroupService, and they have the same version number: 1.0.0. The register information of the service at ConfigServer includes timeout and the serialization pattern. It can be seen from the screenshot that there are 835 machines in the cluster that have subscribed to the service. Some of the subscribers are servers of Taobao (cart is a server that functions as a shopping cart) and some are servers of hitao (taohua).

- 1,328 results are obtained, with 1-20 results displayed on the current page. Retrieval time: 286.794ms
- 835 machines have subscribed to the service, with 63 results displayed on the current page. For detailed information, please refer to: Detailed Data

The HSF system currently deals with more than 30 billion service calls every day.

Some readers may wonder: Now that Taobao has adopted a progressive approach to servitization, how did systems call each other before HSF came into existence?

There were various ways for calling. For example, the calling method used for categories was as follows: Forest was packaged into a JAR file which was then loaded into memory. Such a JAR file required as much as 800MB of memory (because the category data of Taobao was tremendous), which would, after the loading of category data, slow down the running speed of the development machine that had a memory of just 2GB. The first calling method used for the User Information Center (UIC) adopted the Hessian interface. There were other systems which were called via WebService, Socket, or even HTTP requests. Each calling method involved issues concerning timeout, information encryption/decryption, and the definition of parameters, from which we can learn that calls between systems was complicated before the development of HSF. It was in the context of the increasing breakups of systems, which required a unified middle layer to deal with the aforesaid issues, that HSF was developed.

Notify — Message-oriented Middleware

After solving the problem of service calling, let's talk about another problem which has been mentioned before: when a user completes payment through the gateway of a bank, the bank should notify Alipay. However, the bank system may not send the notification to the user; or the user may not receive the notification even if the notification has been sent; or the notification may be sent again even if it has been received by the user. We had long been plagued by the problem. After

Alipay was separated from Taobao, the communication between the two faced the same problem. In 2005, Cheng Li, nicknamed Lu Su (an outstanding strategist and diplomat in the period of the Three Kingdoms of China) suggested we deal with the problem via MQ (message queue), and I was in charge of Taobao's modules for message reading. However, we met a new problem, in that the system frequently suffered from congestion and message sequence error with the increasing number of messages. Besides, messages would get lost if the system broke down, which brought about security concerns. Lu Su then put forward a system-framework-based solution. We stored the notifications which were to be sent in a database. If the system failed to send a real-time notification, the notification would be sent periodically by means of a time program. The system would also keep record of the intermediate state and the time stamp of the message, so that the message was sure to be sent out and the user was sure to be notified. These notifications were arranged in a chronological order, and some of them could even perform transactional operations.

In the wake of the "Qiandao Lake" project and the "wucaishi" project, Taobao's own system was also split into many operational modules, and these modules required similar notifications between each other. For example, when someone bought a product, the transaction management system needed to notify the product management system that it should update its inventory records, notify AliWangWang that it should send WangWang notifications, ask the logistics system to arrange staff to take delivery of the product, inform the SNS system of sharing the order, and report to the system of the public security bureau when there was related fraud. So one request of the user might bring about 10 notifications in the underlying systems. These notifications were called asynchronously (if they were called synchronously, the systems would be coupled and the breakup of the original system would fail) and required a powerful system to support them. In terms of the message volume, these notifications had a larger number than that between Alipay and Taobao. In a similar vein to the "Qiandao Lake" project and the "wucaishi" project, a more powerful message-oriented middleware system was developed and given the name: Notify. Notify is a distributed message-oriented middleware system which is designed to support subscription, sending, and receiving of the messages. The architecture of Notify is shown as follows:

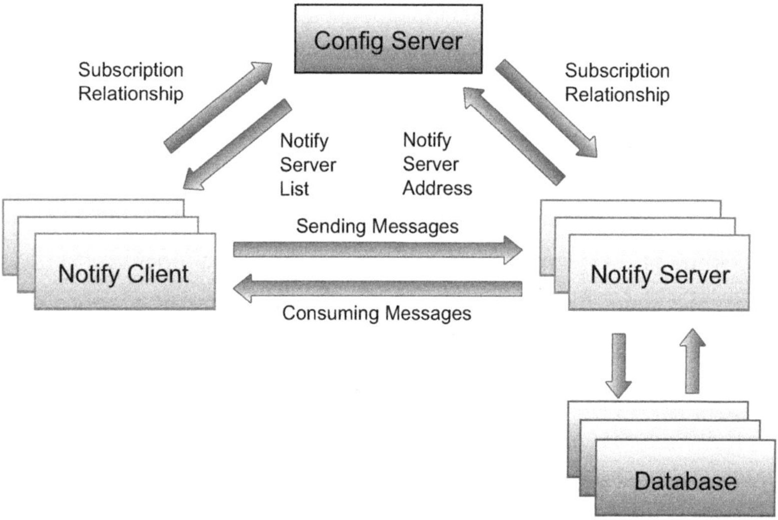

The NotifyServer registers message service on ConfigServer and the client of the message subscribes to the service through ConfigServer. The client then sends a message by calling the NotifyServer which will send the message to all clients that have subscribed to this message (please refer to the section of HSF for its operational principle, which is the same as the principle used here). To ensure that the message can be sent out and that all clients can receive the message, the message data needs to be recorded and stored in a database (any type of database might work). The message has intermediate states (sent, unsent etc.) whereby the application system can achieve distributed transactions — BASE (Basically Available, Soft State and Eventually Consistent). All of the NotifyServer, the NotifyClient and the database can scale horizontally, and therefore, there is theoretically no cap on the throughput of the message system. At present, Notify is dealing with Taobao's daily amount of over 1 billion notifications.

The following diagram shows a series of notifications completed by Notify after the TC (Trade Center) has sent a message to it.

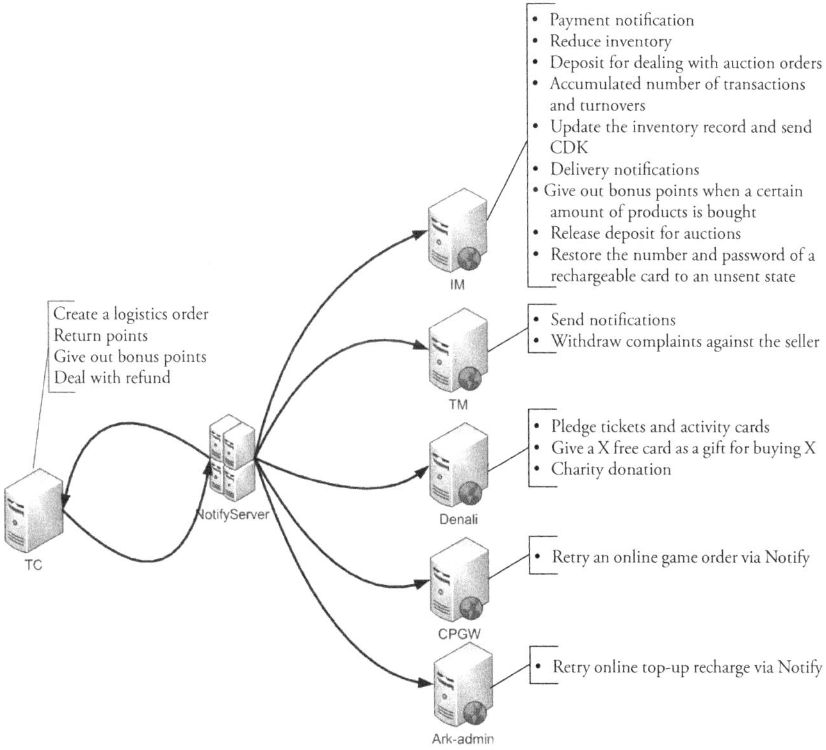

TDDL— a Distributed Data Access Layer

Supported by HSF and Notify, the whole system of Taobao can be separated at the application level. The database, which is a more important factor that restricts the scale of the system, must also be separated.

It has been mentioned in the second part that at a very early time Taobao categorized its databases. The upper-level system connects to a number of databases, and a routing called DBRoute is adopted to pay unified visits to these databases. The DBRoute operates a number of databases and integrates the data, allowing the upper-level system to operate these databases in a way as if it is operating one database. However, as the data volume increases, there are higher requirements for breaking databases down into shards. For example, when you achieve 10 billion-scale product data which cannot be stored in any of the databases, you'll have to break your database down into 2, 4, 8, 16, 32... until 1024, 2048 smaller databases. Well, now that there are so many databases which can accommodate the data, how can we query the data? Some middleware for querying the data is hence required. For the upper-level system, the middleware must be able to query the data in the same way and at the same speed as it does from one database. The TDDL is such middleware.

In addition to data query, functions including data backup, replication and the switch between primary and standby data are all performed in the TDDL. Some systems outside Taobao also name this middleware as DAL (data access layer).

TDDL implements the following three main features:

- Data access routing — transmit read and write requests for data to the most appropriate place;
- Multi-directional and asymmetric data replication — Once

you input the data, it can be read from multiple databases;

- Free extension of data storage —date storage is no longer restricted by the capacity and the speed of one machine, but can be transferred smoothly.

The following graph demonstrates the location of TDDL:

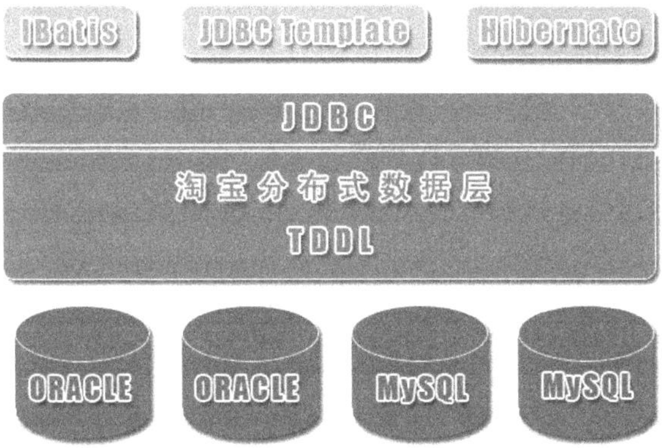

The following graph demonstrates a simple strategy for data query in categorized bases and tables.

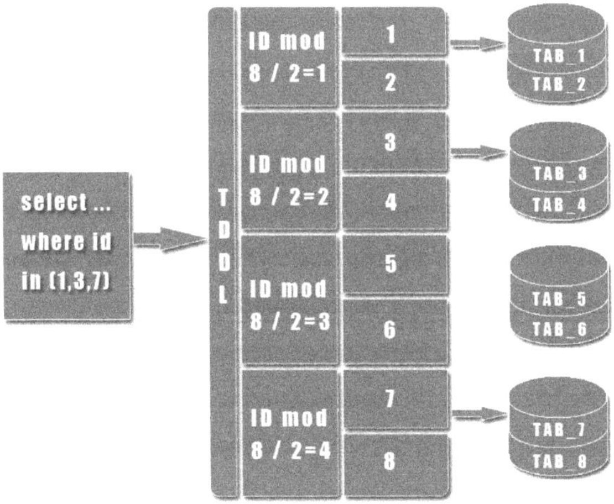

The following part narrated by Shen Xun, one of the main developers of TDDL, is about the "history of TDDL" — the development of the data layer.

• The age of CommonDAO

Data sharding is not a new concept. There had been CommonDAO written by a person called Xingdian (when the product database of Taobao was split into two.

The idea of CommonDAO was very simple and practical. Taobao mainly took ibatis as the DAO layer for visiting databases, and the CommonDAO was adopted to have the ibatis lightly encapsulated, which allowed users to visit either of the databases by virtue of the first character of a product's string ID.

For example, if the first character of the string ID was 0~7, the user would have access to database 1; and if the first character of the string ID was 8~f, the user would have access to database 2. The user was also allowed to visit databases directly by giving the definite name of the databases.

This might have been the earliest prototype of the data layer.

• Era of TDDL 1.0

In view of the scale and speed of service development, we gradually found that it would be difficult to control the cost of the Oracle database which dealt with high-end storage and used minicomputers. Thus, it became necessary to reduce costs.

How could we cut costs to a certain extent without making a negative impact on the development of services?

DBAs decided to apply MySQL on some of the databases. and the burden of designing a distributed data layer fell on Huali.

Although the horizontal sharding of data is common knowledge nowadays, it was a knotty problem for us in 2007 and 2008.

We only knew that eBay had a data layer, but we didn't know how to design or bring to reality such a data layer.

Then we invited heads of various operations to brainstorm what we would demand from the data layer. The results are as follows:

- Achieve unified data access for external users;
- Support caching and file storage systems;
- Switch freely between Oracle and MySQL;
- Support search engines.

Then the problems we met were completely the same with those now asked by people.

How to achieve distributed Join?

After running across the nodes, Join, which had been simple, would become a combination of M×N sets of machines, the cost of which was much higher than that of the original database-based single Join.

How to achieve high-speed multi-dimensional queries?

In the messaging system of SNS, after A sends a message to B, what A wants to see are messages he has sent to others, while what B wants to see are messages he has received from others. How to achieve such a multi-dimensional query in a fast and efficient way?

How to achieve distributed transactions?

There were a large number of transaction operations in the database of the original single machine. Once we established the distributed data layer, the cost of distributed transactions would be much higher than that of transactions executed on a single machine, whereupon the problem would become very prominent.

Huali, Nianbing and I talked about the issue for one and a half months in vain, and we decided to start work first. I named the future data layer Taobao Distributed Data Layer (TDDL, which was dubbed "头都大了"(Tou Dou Da Le) later, meaning "make your head explode" We learned from the open-sourced Amoeba proxy. The target application was "favorites," and the two features that required priority achievement were sharding and the data replication of the heterogeneous database.

We had hoped to cooperate with the B2B team, because we thought that there was no need to create an independent proxy. In addition, subject to special requirements of Taobao, the SQL parser needed to be rewritten.

It's a pity that the B2B team moved to Binjiang (a district in Hangzhou, Zhejiang Province) and it was difficult for us to communicate with each other. As a result, we could only copy and brought nothing new to the open-sourced Amoeba and Cobar at that time.

Back to Taobao, we completed the development of TDDL version 1.0 in slightly more than one month because we had something to refer to. except for some little problems, the release of TDDL was generally successful.

• Era of TDDL 2.0 Era

As TDDL-supported services were in increasing demand, and for service receivers, DBAs gained much experience in using MySQL and data sharding, we decided to work on the core applications.

The first key application was "comment," and the most important issues related to it were two-way query, evaluating, and being evaluated. Thus, the incremental replication of the heterogeneous data source came into play.

The next key application was "product", on which we spent almost half a year. We went through many failures, yet made rapid progress.

- We didn't do capacity planning well, which led to crash of the machine being implemented, as a consequence of overloading. We then created a simulation load testing on database capacity.
- There was a problem left over by history that the design of the interfaces of "product" was complex because almost all services would use "product." It was difficult to call many interfaces at a low cost in the context of the new framework, and much time and cost were required to promote the alteration of services.
- The data layer code was intruded by the service code, resulting in a problem that what was seemingly a piece of data layer code was actually used by "commodity." Such a problem led to growing dependency on the data layer, increasing edge code, and more obvious conflicts between data layer and services.

• Era of TDDL 3.0 – Era of TDDL 4.0

It seemed that we could solve problems caused by the growth of services of almost all applications in a similar way. However, just as we were feeling elated, we suffered a setback in solving problems concerning the application of "transaction."

I always appreciate my colleagues dealing with the "transaction." They are representatives of people who have Taobao's grass-root spirit. They believe that a function may not be that "pretty" but it must have less intermediate links, being practical, clean, and brief. When we introduced our product to them, they had many questions about its implementation details. According to them, only functions like rules and the switch between primary and standby data were useful to them in the process, while functions like parsing and combination were unnecessary.

"Why do you put unnecessary functions in the process? The increased degree of complexity can lead to many problems." I felt rather distressed at that time, because I couldn't answer their doubts.

Nevertheless, it was these doubts that enabled me to review the product I had developed.

I asked myself: how could TDDL benefit our services?

My answer is as follows:

- The rule engine and sharding rules can help services separate the address of a specific database from the service logic of a user by means of configuration;
- Achieve switching between primary and standby data on a single machine;
- Achieve simplification and management of data sources.

We then developed the TDDL version 3.0, the main functions of which were to have the code logically split up into shards, and singled out functions like achieving switching between primary and standby data on a single machine and data source management. In this way, we could conduct logical layering in the light of various demands for services and provide each service with its own way of using databases.

Meanwhile, we started to develop tools and adopted Rtools/JADE as components of the operation and maintenance platform of the database. With the help of Rtools/JADE, we found that users could improve efficiency in using data sources either on a single machine or on multiple machines. Only by defining two properties on the client could users apply these data sources right away. It turned out that we received better user feedback than before.

This, as it were, enhanced our determination to develop tools.

• Era of the Tools Platform

We moved further in tooling components after we benefited from the tools platform.

The first tools platform being established was the "yugong" data migration platform which enabled smooth data migration in various heterogeneous databases, had little impact on services and allowed other services to be inserted into its own logic.

The main functions of the platform were to support services to carry out automatic expansion and contraction of databases and conduct data migration between one single server and multiple servers. The platform also played an important role in the data migration from Oracle to MySQL.

Later, we established the "jingwei" incremental data replication platform via internal open sources. Based on the general data distribution components of the database and the open-sourced Tungsten, the platform carried out a lot of Bug Fix and structural tuning. It also played an important role in one-to-many distribution and sending asynchronous notifications to DW and scenes like searching.

• TDDL at Present

It has been 4 years since TDDL was established. It has met the requirements of nearly 700 service applications, among which there were applications whose core data was related to transactions, products, evaluations, and users as well as less well-known small and medium-sized applications. In terms of the data layer, our key challenge in the future is to meet the requirements of services faster, but at lower cost. The development of TDDL demonstrates the transformation of quantity into quality.

The Session Framework

It is necessary to provide some information about Session before I introduce the Session framework. Session is known as a dialogue in web applications with which we can achieve interactions between the client-side and the service system. HTTP is a stateless protocol, and thus requires Session to maintain the state of the server-side and the browser. After a client sends a first request to a server, the server will establish a Session for it and create a Session token. All the subsequent requests sent by the client shall include this token. The server will proofread the token to identify which Session a request belongs to. By default a dialogue remains valid until the browser is closed.

Data stored in Session include user information, such as the nickname, the User ID, and the log-in state.

When there is just one web server, it is easy to identify the user with Session. However, when there is a cluster of web servers, two requests from the same user may be sent to two servers, which will bring about a problem on how to maintain Session consistency of the two requests. Another problem is that as the website expands, it is inefficient to retrieve user information on the server-side when the Session information of a system that has over 100 million users is stored on the server-side. It takes a lot of memory and CPU time whatever data structure or mechanism the server-side Session adopts. It is a problem as to how to manage the Session information.

Generally there are two solutions to Session sharing in a cluster:

- Hardware load balancing: user requests were sent separately to some specific servers.
- Session replication: replicate the data stored in a user Session to all servers in the cluster.

Disadvantages of the two methods are obvious:

- Relatively high costs.
- Poor performance. The bandwidth increases as the number of PVs increases, and the network load grows exponentially as the number of machines increases. The network lacks high scalability, and the performance declines as servers increase. It might easily cause broadcast storms.

It was under such circumstances that the Tbsession framework was developed. The Tbsession was designed to solve the following issues:

- Client-side storage of Session, which means to store Session information on the client in the form of cookies.
- Implement server-side storage, reduce cookie usage, enhance user information security, and prevent the browser from limiting the number and size of cookies.
- Implement unified management over Session configuration and centralized management over the usage of server-side Session and client-side cookies, and supervise cookie usage.
- Support dynamic update of Session configuration. In short, we are able to login with the help of either client-side cookies

or the Session of the centralized cache region (Tair) on the server-side. I have introduced Tair in the previous part of the book, so I won't repeat it here.

The reason why I still mention the "outdated" Cookie usage is that we had been using Cookie to identify users before Taobao 3.0 was developed. Cookie was stored on the client. Every HTTP request was sent to the server-side. When there were few PVs, the usage of Cookie avoided such problems of high cost as Session replication and hardware overloading. However, the data submitted by a request to a server included both request data sent by a web page and Cookie that had a size of about 2 KB, and the traffic brought about by the Cookie would be considerable when there were over 100 million requests. In addition, the cost of network flow was also increasing. Therefore, we adopted Tair in Taobao 3.0.

So far, supported by the High-Speed Service Framework (HSF), Taobao Distributed Data Layer (TDDL), Message-Oriented Middleware (Notify) and the Session Framework, we have broken up application services (TM, IM), core services (TC, IC), basic services (UIC, Forest) and data storage (DB, TFS, Tair). Taobao 3.0, with its high stability, good scalability, low cost, fast iteration and productized management, entered the history of Taobao technologies.

With the support of the distributed system, more types of business were developed rapidly. Each of them was developed on the basis of such modules as "product", "transaction", "member" and "evaluation" which existed like "clouds" and could be called everywhere. Hitao, Taohua, Liangwuxian, Taobao Mall, eTao, Juhuasuan, various SNS and all kinds of mobile clients mushroomed. At present, Taobao has developed into an "ecosystem" that includes e-commerce related services like C2C, B2C, shopping-guide, group buying and community.

Now that Taobao is a kind of "ecosystem", we should not control all services by ourselves. One of our teams opened Taobao to independent developers when working on Taobao version 3.0, which enabled more developers to call our data and applications through interfaces. These developers could develop all kinds of products. For example, they could develop heart or rhombus-shaped Taobao stores and sell them to sellers on Taobao. Even if Taobao hires countless employees, their creativity is limited; while an "open" Taobao allows numerous people to participate in the development of such an "ecosystem", making the system a complete one.

The following part, narrated by Fangweng who is the architect of the Open Platform, is about Years of Development of the Taobao Open Platform[1].

Taobao Open Platform

At the end of 2006, Alibaba developed the strategy of Work at Alibaba. More than twenty people were called upon to participate in the founding process of Ali Software at Ma Yun's apartment in the Lakeside Gardens. We had a vague understanding of Work at Alibaba then, thinking that it was aimed to provide a working platform for small and medium-sized enterprises. The working platform should be open, because there would be a long tail of needs of the seller. We

1. All technologies mentioned by Fangweng in the text can be found at http://blog.csdn.net/cenwenchu79 for details. This part mainly talks about the development process of the Open Platform, instead of products and services. The target readers are mainly technicians.

were inspired by the Salesforce which was popular then that we could develop a working platform that supported secondary development and could meet the requirements of various sellers for managing the long tail in a semi-open way. The first TPs (Taobao Partner) were fostered to enter the software market then. It was at that time that many of those who are successful TPs today entered the Taobao service market for sellers.

After one year's effort of platform development, however, we found it difficult for developers to perform secondary development through the platform, and only the internal team of Ali Software had developed three different kinds of CRM software. It was at that time that Wang Wenbin (nicknamed Feiqing), who was a master-hand in the industry, came to Taobao. This new chief architect called together members of the platform architecture team of Ali Software, suggesting a kind of technology platform which was very novel at that time: the open platform. Considering that Ali Software had done some similar work, he hoped to cooperate with the company in developing an open platform. They were not sure about the result, and they decided to have one person work for two weeks, seeing if he could work out a prototype of the platform. If he succeeded in doing so, we would move further in platform development; otherwise, we would give up. In the given two weeks, Fangweng, architect of Ali Software, worked out the first prototype of the open platform by referring to the open model of Yahoo, which became the starting point of the following five-year development of the open platform.

Next, I will talk about the product and technological development of the open platform in a chronological order. Many things happened every year, but here are the things that have impressed me the most.

2007: the infancy stage. During the time when SOA prevailed, the opening–up of a platform required servitization of the internal architecture. If internal services were not well isolated, the opening-up would bring about uncontrollable risks. SOFA (similar to ESB) which is the service framework of Alipay, HSF (OSGA) and the ASF of Ali Software (SCA) are all products of that time. However, the attempt of servitization brought about same problems to such service frameworks as OSGI and SCA which had similar servitization design specifications. All architects and developers faced problems in granular control of the service unit Bundle, the management of the dependencies between services, conflicts between performance and specifications and the balance of debugging and isolation. These problems brought about contradictions between frontline developers and implementers of the platform framework. Frameworks that survived the infancy stage abandoned many enterprise-grade design thoughts, because the SOA framework was developed from enterprise-grade products, while the open platform faced by the internal platform after servitization was a product of the Internet.

2008: the prototype stage. At the end of 2008, the platform opened 30 services of Taobao, receiving 2,000 calls every day. The target customers faced by the developers were small- and medium-sized enterprises at Alibaba and individual sellers at Taobao. Three issues needed to be solved at the early stage of the open platform's establishment.

- Service routing (providing independent developers with access to its internal information)
- Standardization of service interfaces (uniform access to various

standardized information)
- Authorization (allowing independent developers to acquire internal information legally)

Service routing is actually the setting of an efficient HttpAgent, and the standardization of service interfaces means the textualization of objects (JSON, XML). The OAuth protocol, which is now widely used by various open platforms, is OAuth 0.6. No actual open Internet platform had applied OAuth until the end of 2008 when Google opened its platform to independent developers and encapsulated OAuth in its Open SDK. It was at that time that many small- and medium-sized Internet companies adopted the seemingly complex two-phase authorization interaction pattern. Taobao used a free agreement at the beginning. It didn't support OAuth2 until 2011 because the former protocol logic of OAuth2 was complex and difficult to use. Meanwhile, it also enhanced data security. The authorization solved the biggest problem in terms of opening-up, which was to enable an application to access to users' data while ensuring user security. Users no longer had to expose their user names and passwords to the application, and developers could make full use of the user authorization to bring new ideas to the application to the extent permitted (concerning operations, data, and duration of authorization).

With the above three supports (routing, data specification, and authorization), the open platform was formally opened to independent developers. The number of daily calls skyrocketed to 1,000 without any previous promotion. Meanwhile, we tried applying two emerging Internet technologies, Memcached and Hadoop to the open platform. The two technologies are widely used nowadays and

Memcached is no doubt the better choice. Memcached, which was known as a distributed memory caching system then, was in fact a kind of centralized memory caching system, and those real distributed memory caching systems were trapped in issues concerning consistency and efficiency (second and third stage submissions). A solution was required at that time to ensure efficiency (scalability) and stability. Therefore, we encapsulated the client-side of Memcached, improved the performance of the client-side of BioJava, and adopted client-side load-balancing and the design for disaster tolerance which is now applied to many large distributed systems. Moreover, with a daily visiting volume of over 10 million, we were required to improve technologies and products to meet the demand for better analysis of access behaviors. Yahoo was making full use of Hadoop then, which attracted our attention (Yahoo played a leading role in technology innovation in the industry then). We tried to create the first internal Hadoop cluster of our company with two machines and a pile of technical documents. We also wrote an introduction to the usage of Hadoop which became a primer for the usage of Hadoop at that time. Hadoop could easily meet the demand for log analysis of the 2,000 calls every day. However, problems caused by Hadoop offline analysis were highlighted as a result of the constant service development. With diverse demands for analysis, the MR program became inefficient and difficult to maintain, which required us to think about how to improve the Hadoop.

2009: the productization stage. By the end of 2009, over 100 Taobao services had been opened to independent developers through the platform, with 4,000 daily calls. In 2009, the developers of the open platform developed products mainly for Taobao's individual sellers, and tools for sellers became mainstream products on the service market. The year 2009 also saw the spin-off of AliSoft, which led to the problem in regard to the ownership of the open platform. One choice was to keep the platform in the new company Aliyun, making the platform serve as a basic facility of the Group; the second choice was to make it part of Taobao which was the main party to use the open platform. We finally persuaded Doctor to shut down the old platform of AliSoft, and henceforth Taobao formally began its "opening-up." The number of services grew rapidly with APIs increasing from 30 to 100, and the call volume, even without any promotion, had doubled by the end of 2009. We then focused on improving the performance of the platform. It took about 30–40ms to perform an API call, and it took about 10ms on average for the platform to process a call. We conducted data management and analysis, finding that it took us the longest time to accept internet data, and the large amount of image data further increased the processing time of the platform. Moreover, after analyzing the access log, we found that many invalid requests also took a lot of processing time, meaning that both invalid and valid requests were consuming the limited thread resources containers. Therefore, we began to try to encapsulate byte stream parsing modules by ourselves and analyze upstream data as required, which on one hand improved the performance of data analysis (the analysis of parallel services and data increments), and on the other allowed the platform to handle exception requests at the lowest cost (all subsequent data would be abandoned if there was a request that didn't meet the service specification). All these were achieved by the LazyParser with a focus on parsing parallel services and data while minimizing data caching. The LazyParser worked well after it being released, and the average processing time dropped from 10ms to

4ms. (The time included the improvement of exception handling and parsing performance.)

On the other hand, problems related to the Hadoop MR became increasingly prominent, which was followed by issues in regards to the maintenance cost and performance of the MR Class. We then tried to conduct an abstract analysis of service scenarios, thinking about whether we could achieve the various functions for statistical analysis by configuration. The substitution of code with configuration depended on whether we could exhaust all possible statistical functions achieved by code. After reviewing the concepts of SQL, we found that all statistics, when they were split into KV for input and output, required the functions Max, Min, Average, Sum, Count, and Distinct (which was achieved in 2012 by using bloomfilter and AtomicLong), or a bit more complex, the mathematical expressions of the results of these functions. After abstracting discrete statistics configuration functions for KV input and output, we grouped sets of KV by the Key, which led to the conventional statement (K, v1, v2…). After that, the daily statistics functions could be changed by configuration without the need of a large number of MR codes. In addition, all analyses could be completely handled by only one attempt of data input, and the performance was substantially improved.

Hadoop analyzed and abstracted model configuration, which solved problems in terms of performance and usability. Nevertheless, it didn't apply to real-time analysis. We hoped to complete an incremental analysis of data within one hour, so as to monitor the overall condition of service calling and guarantee real-time check for exceptions. The platform received 4000 calls every day. Considering that it was not a very large number, we thought about adopting a sharding approach that used MySQL and creating SQL queries at regular time. We received good results after doing so. A component was also created in the process. On one hand, writing log data to the disk and the database required many I/O interfaces, and on the other, it was nothing serious to lose some log records because the MySQL was not a system for financial management. In such cases, we adopted asynchronous writing of bulk data to external storage (each of the multiple threads took charge of its own buffer, refreshing the external storage at regular time or in full-page), whereby, the load of a single machine didn't exceed 0.7 when the log data were written to both the disk and the database.

By late 2009, however, we met a problem which became an "invisible bomb" of the open platform. One night, there were warnings of large-scale denial of services of the platform. After examining the whole cluster, we found that the processing time for services increased to 1s from the original average time of 30-40ms. We examined more closely and found that the response time needed by a certain service rose sharply, with the time skyrocketing from 20ms to over 1s. At that time, HTTP requests were submitted synchronously, which caused a slow release of the cluster thread of the front-end service routing gateway and then blocked requests for processing the service; in addition, other normal services (services behind the Taobao Open Platform were maintained by different teams, and the processing time for these services varied from 1ms to 200ms) were denied access. Both conditions led to the aforesaid warnings. A moment later we found that the time increased because the team that took charge of the certain service had failed to create a database index. The problem upset the open platform from time to time, and we found it unacceptable to have the stability of the platform be subject to any services. To solve this problem, we first thought about splitting the cluster into important services and unimportant services, but we gave up the idea in consideration of the cost (the utilization rates of different services varies greatly) and the possibility that services might not be separated thoroughly (important services would influence each other).We then came up with the idea of using Haproxy and LVS, both of which were load balancing software. Haproxy was a layer 7 load balancer while LVS was a layer 4 load balancer. We considered using the former because the load balancing involved services and tried running one Haproxy on 7 virtual machines. We could carry out dynamic adjustment during the operation and balance traffic by manual intervention when the configuration went wrong. Henceforth, we could intervene with semi-manual balancing when there was a warning. Although we solved the problem, we still didn't feel relieved. We had thought of sending web requests in an asynchronous manner and using the Servlet3 model to avoid platform block caused by synchronous HTTP requests. However, after conducting stress testing on Jetty and Tomcat, which were the only two web servers that supported Servlet3 at that time, we found the results were unstable.

2010: the platform stage. By the end of 2010, over 300 Taobao services had been opened to independent developers through the platform, with a daily calling volume of 800 million. It was in 2010 that Taobao formally kicked off the promotion of its "opening-up," which proved to be a success. Many TPs who have an annual income of over 10 million were "pioneers" at that time (they were seen as "martyrs" before 2010). In terms of products, the year 2010 saw a continuous development of tools for sellers. It also saw that the popularity of SNS gave rise to applications for buyers at Tao

Jianghu (a social network of Taobao) and seekers looking for game applications streamed in the platform. In addition, the number of services opened through the platform kept a growth rate of 300% in 2010, and services were no longer designed only for sellers, but also for buyers. Starting with the offering of API, the website of Taobao was able to support the usage of deeply integrated applications in Taobao stores and communities in 2010.

Faced with a volume of 800 million visits, it was no longer possible to conduct streaming data analysis with MySQL. What's more, the time required for the analysis was shortened from one hour to 20 minutes. We had learned and applied the Hadoop for almost one and a half years then, and gained a systematic understanding of the distributed system. Therefore, we started to develop the first version of streaming analysis system. We kept MR for abstracting while adopting another method for low-level data analysis and calculations. Thermometer method is different from Hadoop in that:

- The task data being analyzed comes from the remote server log (via Pull technology, instead of Push technology).
- It conducts passive task allocation and task scheduling (which are similar to the Volunteer Computing mode); performs lightweight task management via Master and requires Slave to perform tasks once it is added; doesn't monitor task performance; resets the condition of a task only by timeout.
- It uses Master to reduce tasks in a unified manner whereas Slave can support shuffling to decrease the data transmission volume and the stress of combination between Master and Slave; Master functions to send outputs to locals in a unified manner.

In general, data sources changed. The calculation interactions between data nodes were not performed by means of disk files (they would be discarded after only one use in memory), and both task scheduling and data merge were simplified. The first version of streaming analysis was thus developed. It was constantly improving because of challenges met by the aforesaid designs, and we found similar practices in the designs of Hadoop and Hive. The three virtual machines of the system fulfilled 800 million real-time log analyses. This was the end of the part of MySQL log analysis.

Another significant change in 2010 was that more people recognized the value of the platform opening-up, and we witnessed the extension from department opening-up to the opening-up of Taobao as a whole. In the next part, I will explain what departmental opening-up is. A decade ago, the opening-up of most APIs was encapsulated and maintained by the team that took charge of the open platform. The team had plenty of time and energy to manage 30 APIs, yet it was overwhelmed by 100 APIs (It must be admitted that members of the team have the most comprehensive professional knowledge ofTaobao at present).When there were over 300 APIs, it became impossible for just one team to manage them, and we received frequent complaints for interface instability, which was caused by service change. To solve the problem, we launched the "Long March Project" on lightweight services, whereby we accessed services in an automated manner by means of tools and the platform. In addition, the process in which a service was launched in a point-to-point manner in one week was simplified, and one could launch a service in one day with the help of the automated service publication platform. What's more, SD Ks could be generated automatically in various languages. All these, as it were, provided a foundation for lightweight services. We then accessed newly-developed services in this pattern and returned the old services to service receivers for maintenance. The "stability" of services (in terms of business) was thus significantly improved, and a noticeable increase was seen in user satisfaction.

Nevertheless, problems were always emerging one after another. The problem, which has been mentioned earlier, that the instability of the background applications would lead to an unstable platform which occurred more frequently after the launch of the lightweight services, because both service publication and maintenance were performed by departments being in charge of back-end operations. In that case, the control of the various systems became weaker and the stability indicators of the KPIs basically could not be ensured. The only way to completely solve the problem was to introduce asynchronous HTTP services, an event-driven model and a separate virtual thread pool. In the middle of 2010, we conducted stress testing on Jetty 7, finding that the Continuations could be implemented in a formal environment. We then encapsulated the asynchronous HTTP services and the event driven model on the basis of Jetty7, and meanwhile, achieved a separate virtual thread pool to support them. I won't go further here, but the principles can be briefly described as follows:

- Separate the front-end container thread from transaction processing. (It is similar to the differences between NIO and BIO)
- If the transaction processing is dependent on an external system, an event-driven approach will be adopted to reduce the time for a thread to wait for an event, and meanwhile, to increase the utilization rate of resources occupied by threads.

Here we can see many differences in the details. We decided whether an event-driven approach was required according to the ratio of the time consumed by the external system to the total time. In addition, the event-driven approach brought about large amount of resource consumption due to switching.

- Set the largest amount of resources that can be consumed by different transactions by means of a large thread pool in a virtual manner, so as to fully share resources and prevent transactions from occupying too many resources when there is an exception (the transactions queue up to be processed, instead of occupying too many resources).

Several days after the component release, there followed a typical case. At 2 pm, the response time of a service increased from 10ms to 40ms, and then to 200ms. The largest number of threads that we had set in simulation for the service was 20 at that time, and we found that the threads released slowly and were used up gradually because of the increase in RT, which led to the increase of transactions that waited for processing from 0 to 100, and then, to 200... (To avoid occupying too much memory, transactions that surpassed the queue length would be discarded.) Meanwhile, other transactions were using the resources as usual and the platform was running smoothly. After 4 pm, the problem was fixed after service receivers had been informed of warnings. The RT decreased to 10ms and requests that had been waiting for processing also began to decrease, and finally, the queue was empty and the occupation of threads return to normal level again.

After that, Zhenzi said to me happily that he could write 9s at will to the stability KPI of the open platform.

2011: the marketization stage. By the end of 2011, 758 Taobao services had been opened to independent developers through the platform with1.9 billion calls per day. In 2011, the SNS fervor was ebbing away and game applications were found on the margins, yet the service market for sellers still went on well with marketing tools showing up, becoming the new favorites of developers. What's more, the Taobaoke contributed a lot to the open platform (In 2011, both Fanli and group buying gained popularity. The difference was that the former returned money to customers while the later got the customers to blow money).

As the open platform was generally believed to have a promising future, a "blasting fuse" appeared leading to transformation and contraction of the opening-up. Tuangoubao, a company dealing with tool marketing, synchronized the information of some discounted products set by sellers to Taobao through the interface in the early morning every day. One day before dawn, someone posted it on Weibo that some Taobao shops were full of cheap products at the price of 1 yuan. Many products were soon bought at this price because such a piece of news was widely-spread and far-reaching at that time when Weibo was popular. It was found out later that prices of offline products were all modified to 1 yuan with unknown reasons, and the above situation occurred after synchronization before dawn. Since then, security was given the top priority for KPI of the open platform, and the subsequent technology products were also centered on security. The first system that had to be improved was the streaming analysis cluster. Its time for data analysis was shortened from 20 minutes to 3 minutes and the daily data volume increased from 800 million to 1.9 billion. I spent two months off and on in optimizing the structural design of cluster and processing capacity of the single machine. I won't go further here because a similar situation was detected when I looked over the optimization process of Hadoop. In short, the following four aspects are included: making full use of multi-core capacity to save memory with computing; saving memory with disk and adopting a concurrent design to maintain the overall processing time or even reduce it; using Slave Shuffle to reduce the combined stress of Master and Slave; conducting data compression to reduce consumption of data transmission and memory usage.

Now that we gained full understanding of and encapsulated Jetty7 in 2010, we saw an opportunity for another new technology. I saw the function of Comet being realized with Jetty 7 by some foreigners during JavaOne 2010. At first, Comet was primarily used to transfer the application with CS structure to the Internet. As we couldn't use TCP persistent connection, we adopted the HTTP persistent connection to replace the original mode. Foreign open platforms were also concerned with new API designs including Streaming API from Twitter, which meant to push messages to an external ISV (Independent Software Vendor) through HTTP persistent connection. Attracted by this model, we decided to further upgrade the encapsulation of Jetty 7 so as to support Comet persistent connection. Meanwhile, the back-end actively pushed messages from internal to external through the event-driven mode in order to avoid the external polling service interface. The key of the design was to use the most effective and fewest threads to guard multiple persistent connections and support the event-driven data downlink to the back-end. If a data push daemon thread was used to support each persistent connection, the highest immediacy can be achieved at the cost of consuming numerous daemon threads with vacant connection. This mode was surrounded by all kinds of doubt after it came into being. People thought it was wickedly offbeat, as it did away with the common practice (using Pull) and wouldn't be accepted by developers for being unstable. However, several dauntless developers supported high-speed processing of several million orders with only one PC during the "Double 11" festival in 2011, showing that we should dare to develop new technologies, write code, and delve into details, because nothing is impossible. From then on, diversified services such as TQL, Schedule API, and ATS emerged through the open platform, providing various solutions and innovations for more scenarios and terminals.

2012: the verticalization stage. From 2012 to the present, there are over 900 Taobao services opened through the platform with 2.5 billion calls every day. Taobao changed its orientation in 2012, which led to the decrease in popularity of Taobaoke. Wireless business mushroomed. New services (including services of plane tickets, lottery, hotel, financing, etc.), P4P and data services began to operate API, and the customer groups of open platform developers extended from individual sellers to brand companies and distributors of Taobao Mall.

This year was stamped by changes in business and marked a new stage of approval for the employees of Taobao. The first stage was to allow the department of the open platform to conduct opening-up and encapsulation at will. The second stage was to make service receivers take charge of open services, the result of which was unknown and didn't need to be known. At the third stage, services were required to be opened actively, after which we operated the services, cultivated the ISV market, and led positive development of services.

Because of the increase in service volume and the requirements for analysis of the user dimension, the project of reconfiguring and upgrading streaming analysis clusters was launched at the end of 2011. The project was named Beetles because we hoped that it could work as a beetle which can eat as many leaves as possible. It took us about two and a half months (from the end of 2011 to the beginning of 2012) to conduct a complete configuration, during which we redesigned the old code and drew on the experiences collected in these years in patching. We also implemented vertical sharding of Master according to services, which finally solved the problem of combined pressure on the Master. There was no doubt that we conducted much technology optimization. For example, our goal was to reduce the time from 3 minute to 1 minute, to double the data volume and to refine the statistical dimension to the user dimension. (It implies big results. How could we achieve more partitioning and collaborative designs if we didn't conduct transfers with files?)

This year witnessed two innovative projects, namely JS SDK and Wireless SDK (IOS and Android versions), both of which were determined to some extent by service and security. First, the project of community e-commerce (now the XTao project) was launched at the end of 2011, connecting more websites with Taobao. It required lighter and simpler integration between websites, and Facebook provided a successful case for us on this matter. At the beginning of 2012, I began to write codes after looking through JS SDK of Facebook. With the help of UED, JS SDK became more reliable and professional. Meanwhile, JS SDK ensured the service security of buyers because previously it was impossible to know whether a REST call was conducted by the user or the server after authorization, while JS SDK could verify the validity of Cookie so as to ensure the presence and knowing of users to some extent. The wireless SDK in the second half of the year was a product which was developed after reading various documents for a month. With the widespread use of Java language, dynamic language, and scripting language, it was not that difficult to learn Objective-C language. We could also deal with things on the SDK base layer smoothly because it didn't involve too much MVC knowledge. The IOS version of wireless SDK was thus created. At the same time, we launched the Hack project inside the technical team of open platform, among which one of the independent sub-projects was developing an Android version of wireless SDK. The version was developed successfully after one month. Both versions of the wireless SDK are responsible for managing wireless security issues. In fact, many companies in the industry, including Taobao, didn't realize the big risk of wireless, and OAuth2 could not ensure the security of wireless users. Therefore, the first key demand for wireless SDK was to integrate the security design of higher levels with SDK and the server.

In 2012, we focused on the construction of a security system of the open platform and conducted all-around control over security from the following two aspects:

The first was for users. For user authorization, the operation range of authorization (bringing granularity to data category) and authorization duration were refined. All information can be monitored, filed, and located quickly. Inside Taobao, we called it Top Ocean. Briefly speaking, it filed all access logs with file blocks and set indexes for all records of the file blocks as required during filing. These indexes were then saved. In addition, local files were uploaded to a remote distributed file system as backups, and real-time monitoring was conducted to service calls and application access, which enabled authorization transactions.

The second was for third-party applications. Monitoring clusters were used to conduct security scanning of all ISV servers, scanning of common Web security holes and monitoring of applications on their availability and response time. Meanwhile, we formally launched the "Jushita" project to provide ISV with elastic computing and storage capacity as well as a secure network environment, helping ISV ensure security of its own applications.

Now we have shown you part of the development of Taobao technologies during the past 5 years, which just includes the typical ones. Meanwhile technical development is only part of the development of the open platform. The past 5 years have witnessed a development driven by technological reform, whereas the 5 years yet to come will be a period marked by a development fueled by changes in business and our understanding of services. The value of the open platform is directly based on our understanding of services. I have touched on the ups and downs of various open services during the 5 years, and in fact, there were more intriguing stories behind the scenes. After 5 years of development, Taobao now consists of Taobao marketplace (C2C), T-mall (B2C), eTao (an entrance for searching and rebates in e-commerce), wireless services, new services, O2O (local life) and a group-buying platform (Juhuasuan). What are the values of these platforms? How should they find their orientations? How to develop Taobao with the help of external forces? How to cope with the rise of the flow entrance, the e-commercialization of traditional online enterprises and the competition between e-commerce platforms? These are the highlights of the open platform in 2012 and in the next 5 years.

CHAPTER 6

My Eight Years in Taobao

As a participant of the growth of Taobao technologies, I became an unwitting witness of a great history, which seems magnificent from the perspective of the executives, an interesting and amazing from the viewpoint of the grassroots employees. I'm not a senior executive, and what I write down here is something that happened among the staff members.

It was not until some co-workers said congratulations to me on December 8, 2011 that I realized it had been seven years since I joined Taobao. I was often asked, "Do you feel the seven-year itch?" To be honest, I did, but only for a second. And after that I threw myself into the abyss of work. I asked myself when I got home: what on earth did I get from these seven years. Regardless of success or failure, my experience through these seven years is a valuable asset of my life.

The First Year (2004–2005)

Zhengpai Qigong (@正牌七公) once said that if he was to write a book about the history of Taobao, it would definitely arouse a lot of people's interest. Actually I wanted to write such a book myself. When I came to the company on December 8, 2004 together with Nazi Ruhuan (@衲子如幻), we were greeted by Luo Bing and Huang Shang (@岳旭强). Luo Bing was the head teacher of the Hundred-year Alibaba training course, and Huang Shang was my tutor. There was no Hundred-year Taobao at that time. So I took the Hundred-year Alibaba training course first, and received a book named *The Perfect Store*, which introduced stories of eBay. When I was reading the book, it came up to me that maybe someday I can write a book about the stories of Taobao.

I joined Taobao quite by chance. Back when I was getting tired of doing outsourced work of Japanese companies, I accidentally noticed this website and found it well-designed, and I made up my mind to apply for a job at Taobao. I was pretty much shocked when I walked in the company. It seemed quite different from those traditional companies, as everyone here looked so vibrant and vigorous, and the receptionist A Good Friend of Xiangxiang (@香香的好朋友) always wore a friendly, warm smile on her face when she talked with me, while most receptionists I met in other companies were always as cold as stone. Wudang Sanfeng (@武当三丰) gave me two sheets of questions as a quiz, and to my surprise, I passed it. When God of Wealth gave me an interview and asked why I applied to Taobao, I replied that a company that grew this fast must had a lot of real experts, together with whom I could also grow quickly. He nodded to whatever I said with an "uh-huh." He did so much of it that when I described the company CEO to my wife later, she could only remember a guy that "Uh-huh" a lot.

The first task I undertook in Taobao was Java development, but I only had three months' experience in doing this, and not even familiar with Eclipse (I boned up on shortcut key operation before I came in). I worked under the hand-holding guidance of Yue Xuqiang (@岳旭强) at first, and received a lot of help from senior associates who sat near me—Duolong, Zhengfeng, Jinbao, Woxing, Butong, Fanyu and Tianchuan. There were no ready-to-use process for us to follow at the time. What we usually did was checking out what function the users needed in the forum, and asked the PD if it was necessary. If so, we would write codes and submitted them for testing (by Zizai, Guofu and Baoju), packaging (by Qingqing), and launching (by Jianying). I still remember clearly that the first requirement came from a seller who did not want to sell to buyers with credibility lower than one heart. For sellers who did not want to sell to buyers in specific provinces, I developed a tool to restrict access of certain buyers. I added some parameters and a few lines of codes in the process of commodity release and order generation before I had them uploaded.

This function was not put into use after uploading. Three years later, this piece of code was still there unused until Denali was about to be split in 2008.

My confidence was boosted by the fact that I finished the first task successfully and had my codes running on the system. In the meantime, HR was operating a project called Hundred-year Taobao. I attended the second course of Hundred-year Taobao for a couple of days (I was too busy when asked to take the first course in the first place. So I had to put off the training and attend the second course. Over a hundred courses have been held in Hundred-year Taobao till now), and found myself involved in a more awesome project—Alipay.

Alipay was born on the Taobao system. At the end of 2004, Jack Ma saw the potential of Alipay with his keen insight. He turned to Sun Microsystems to convert Taobao's original PHP architecture into Java architecture and develop an independent Alipay system. Tianchuan and I were relocated to Alipay and took charge of Taobao-related business. Besides people from Sun and two of us from Taobao, a major figure joined the team as DBA of the project. I still remember that when he first came to Hangzhou, he contacted the local ISP for broadband installation in his house only to be provoked by their poor service. He blamed the ISP for a long time and was very much experienced at dealing with such conditions when arguing with China Telecom on Weibo later on (2010). There were some other heavyweights that I admired a lot in the project team—like Lu Su and Miao Renfeng, who became Chief

System Architect and Business Architect of Alipay later. So I worked for three months with these veterans and launched Alipay on May Day. The tired-looking faces of DBAs who worked on data migration are still fresh and vivid in my mind. The data structure changed so dramatically that @Zhengpai Qigong, @fenng, Duolong, Lu Su and I had to work for three days and nights straight. As we stayed up all night, some sellers came from Hangzhou to visit us. One of them was Bijun, who joined Taobao later.

Those days of burning passion remain to be an abiding memory of mine. My wife called me up when I stayed at work for three days and nights, asking me "Do you still love me or not?" I replied, "How could I not love you?"

During my first year at Taobao, my grade was P1 (which does not exist today), corresponding to today's P3. By the end of the year, Sanfeng gave me a score of 4 (beyond expectation) and promoted me to P4. That was a period that marked my fastest growth.

The Second Year (2005–2006)

When the development of Alipay was completed, the company held a huge celebration ceremony and arranged a trip to the Qiandao Lake for us. We did have a lot of fun there, but I felt a little bit uneasy, as I had been working with them for only 3 months, and created only three functions—the interface for creating Alipay transactions, the interface for receiving Alipay order status, and the function for binding and unbinding an Alipay account, whereas the other on the team established a significant system, impressing me deeply. Six months later, Taobao organized another trip to the Qiandao Lake. And later we went to the Qiandao Lake two more times for celebration of another two projects. We have been there for so many times that I can even find my way about.

Back from the Qiandao Lake, the real hard work started. For a long time I was busy with the debugging of the Alipay system. Since Alipay and Taobao were two separate systems, communication between the two could be a big problem. In addition, Alipay also needed to communicate with banks, so problems occur frequently: when users made bank transfer payments, Alipay might not be notified of the payment, and even if Alipay received the notification, it might not be able to notify Taobao. So the users paid the money but the transactions were not updated and the payments were not shown on Taobao, which was very frustrating. Lu Su and I tried a variety of ways, starting with MQ (what is this?). But messages were often lost and the time sequences were wrong when concurrency went up. Then he set up a messaging middleware system, which was the prototype of Taobao Notify. Today Notify deals with hundreds of millions of messages per day and makes sure that every message is delivered in proper time sequence without duplication, which was a difficult task.

Sanfeng noticed that I had done a lot of work in Alipay and cooperated well with Lu Su and other team members, thinking that I had made great progress. So I got a promotion to PM (project manager) while carrying on maintenance of Alipay interface at the same time. Some said that I was Taobao's first PM, to which I felt a great honor. I sorted out and developed with the SQA some groundbreaking works such as Project Management Process, PM Workbook, and System Design Templates, some of which are still in use. But later when the concept of Agile Development was proposed, I couldn't help thinking that whether I had exerted a misleading influence on Taobao's model of project development for many years.

My career as a PM lasted from 2005 to 2008, basically divided into two stages—the "novice" stage, when I had to fly by the seat of my pants with several projects, including Commodity Details Split, Favorites Reform, and Alipay Authentication, and the tough battle stage, as I threw myself into the development of My Taobao AJAX Edition, Zhaocaijinbao, and Taobao Trip. Why was it a tough battle? It was because two of these three projects failed and only one survived.

Commodity Details Split started in 2005 when Sanfeng wanted me to be the project manager. I felt apprehensive and uncertain for the title of manager, but was told that there were only two members in the project team—Tolui and I. What we needed to do was quite simple. The Taobao commodity information sheet was a table from the outset, and all the information was contained in the table, including commodity details, and stored as a clob (a data type used by various database management systems, including Oracle and DB2, storing large amounts of character data up to 4 GB) field. As everyone knows, commodity details could be a field of dreadful length. It is said that the Taobao commodity details sheet would be about 5 meters long in average when printed out. Of course it was not so long at that time, but it was scary enough. It would jeopardize the read and write performance of data when stored together with other information. So I created a table to store the commodity details, which was only accessible in commodity details sheet rather than general commodity query. The performance was significantly enhanced when the project was done, and it made me feel proud for a long time. Later on commodity details were no longer stored in the database but in the file system instead.

Favorites Reform was a larger and more complicated project. Wanjian, Lingjun, and I gave it our all to turn the original Favorites into a multi-functional collection of commodities, stores, and search results that could be sorted as desired. The UI of the new Favorites was designed by Chengzhi @sharkUI pixel by pixel, which seems even fatiguing than code writing. This project was a relatively comprehensive process to me, as I took charge of work planning and even project management document preparation, in addition to code writing.

Alipay Authentication was an innovation of Taobao, which, as early as upon its establishment, required the sellers to submit photos of their Chinese ID card for real-name authentication and connected to the website of the public security system to verify the identity information at a high cost of RMB 5 per user. Qianxue (@浅的雪) joined the team as a PD later and proposed a new way of authentication: we believed that the banks must have identity information of their clients, and now that Alipay had a cooperation relationship with the banks, it was possible to verify the users' identity via the client information of the banks. In other words, the principle of Alipay Authentication was: users give us their identity information and bank accounts and we deposit some money into their accounts. Then the users fill in the amount of money they received (we claimed to deposit a sum of money less than RMB 1, but in fact only a few cents). If the number they fill in matches with the money we deposit, the identity of this person is true. This approach not only reduced the costs of authentication, but also shortened the authentication period from a week to one day. Since I was

familiar with Alipay and had served as a PM before, I took over this project as a PM as a matter of course. I was told that the project applied for a patent later, which was a great innovation indeed.

I considered myself a qualified project manager after the success of these three projects, but some big failures awaited me in the near future. I had better stop writing right here, since what happened later was too sad to think about.

The Third Year (2006–2007)

I got married at the end of 2005 when I was responsible of a larger project – reconstruction of the My Taobao. After registering for marriage at the Civil Affairs Bureau, I rushed back to the company in such a hurry that my marriage certificate was lost on the way. Fortunately someone found the certificate and returned it to the Bureau. This is why I went to the Bureau for the marriage certificate twice in one day.

My Taobao was a functional area where Taobao members managed their products, transactions, delivery addresses, reviews, and complaints. As this area was only visible after logging in, it used to have a completely different style and interface, and hadn't been optimized for a long time. The interface was ugly and inconvenient for user operation. If a seller had lots of products, he had to operate them one by one when he wanted to release them or remove them off the shelves. That was really troublesome (think about the book sellers). At that time, an important figure came, and that was Chengzhi (@ SharkUI). He demonstrated to us the most advanced front-end interaction technique, just like the interactive AJAX of Gmail. You can drag, use the right mouse button, or employ composite keys.

And you needn't refresh the page when an operation is completed. It's an amazing technique for the management of products. Besides Chengzhi, we had another professional in the team, Yideng (@喻策), and that was his first project as a PD. We kicked off the project together with Wanjian and a group of engineers. I named the project "Alps" like the mountain range. The foreground project of Taobao was called Denali, and the background project was called McKinley, both of which were named after famous mountains. So we needed to use the name of a more famous mountain for our project. During the project, I changed the desktop wallpaper to a picture of Alps, and bought Alpenliebe Swiss candy for my co-workers while they worked overtime. Everyone was in high spirits. When we were about to finish, Jack Ma suddenly showed up behind me. After watching me running the new version of My Taobao, he asked me whether it was a piece of client-end software. He went nuts when I told him that it was a web page, saying that it was the same as client-end software without even an underline beneath the links and using file folders for the release and removal of products. He said even he didn't know how to use it, let alone the sellers. We were not convinced but took his advice with a grain of salt. So we created a beta version and released it so that some users can experience the new version first hand.

Before long, the first mass disturbance in Taobao's history broke out. After trying the new version of My Taobao, many sellers went mad, saying they didn't know how to use it. Yideng and Chengzhi worked together trying to modify the page into one that was closer to a web page. After half a month's trial, the sellers' anger remained. Seeing the two of them hanging there, I was frustrated and talked with the supervisors for a solution. Then we put up a vote on the forum about whether the new version of My Taobao should be used and the result showed over a half of the voters against it. So the system that had taken three months' hard work of a dozen people was summarily killed. All I could feel at that point was shame and guilt for my pals and the paychecks I received during the three months. But what pained us most was, after the new version was halted, some sellers got angry, saying how could such a great function be canceled.

Although the supervisors did not blame me for the failure of My Taobao AJAX Edition project, I was so engaged in remorse and self-reproving that I summed up several major mistakes I made during the project as an object lesson, which could relieve my regret. On May 1, 2006, another epoch-making project was launched (sadly I lost two May Day Holidays). The God of Wealth said the project needed the best and strongest team and I was selected. That I was classified into the category of the best employees cured my heart injured during the previous project. It was a P4P system for commodities. With this system, sellers paid per deal. We thought many sellers had earned money and they would be willing to pay for their products to be ranked in the front rows, since there were so many products on Taobao and it was very difficult to locate one. We allowed sellers to buy advertisement spaces and ranked their products based on a certain algorithm (similar to Baidu's search engine ranking system, but not only depended how much a seller paid, but also the credit, transaction volume, and Favorites collection amount, resulting in an extremely complex algorithm). What a wonderful profit-earning pattern it could be! Within our strong team, Qiao Feng (@王煜磊) was the service receiver, Qianxue was PD, Huangshang, Jinbao, Xiaofeng, and Changkong were programmers, Zizai and Feiyan were testers, Qingtong and @sharkUI were UEDs, Xingdian was the architect, and Yekai was DBA.

In our development process, Qiao Feng broke his leg when playing football and had to work in SOHO. As often as not, he would encourage me a lot from the other end of the network. It was the first time I heard the word SOHO, but in his case SOHO represented being in a hospital instead of at home. This system went on smoothly, but when it was released, a bigger mass disturbance broke out. The sellers questioned, "Haven't you promised that you won't charge any fees in three years? Doesn't the advertising cost count?" Then our competitors fueled the disturbance, making stirs in various social networks, and one competing company even put forward a "mass destruction" function of "one click move" together with the Taobao credits. Again the project ended in failure. On the day that the project went offline, Qiao Feng burst into tears first. The God of Wealth told him to be a true man who knows when to hold on and when to let go. We went to Xuzhu's home in the evening for dinner as a closure of the project. The God of Wealth got drunk after only two shots of spirits. I didn't eat much because the others didn't feel like eating at all. At the end, Xiaobao and I took him home when dinner was over. Xiaobao, who was physically stronger than me, carried him on the back, while I held the umbrella and walked by their side. On that night, the street lights were misty and there was a lasting drizzle.

Some said that the failure of this project delayed the maturity of China's e-commerce for years, but the people who kicked us when we were down didn't get anything good.

After two successive failures, I was relieved from sorrow. With a relaxed attitude, I realized the fact that a person was not meant to succeed if he tried hard. As an old saying goes, "Man proposes, God disposes."

I did a good deal of work on other regular jobs, the most impressive being was a demand from Fat Hu Fei for a lottery system at the year end. According to what he said, the system should be able to draw the lottery instantly when the number of lottery buyers could be estimated. The prizes should be evenly distributed in a day within a preset limit, with none left. What a dilemma he put me into! After a lot of thought, I came up with an algorithm using a random number as the seed of lottery. The lottery buyer won only when number fell into a certain interval, and the amount of awards were limited within an hour. When all the awards were given out, those numbers that fell into the set interval would not win. If the awards were given out too soon during the previous hour, the winning interval would be narrowed down. This algorithm was later applied to many lotteries.

When the heartbreaking third year came to an end, I was already a P5 employee.

The Fourth Year (2007–2008)

When Good Fortune failed during the fourth year (2007-2008), Qiao Feng almost cried his eyes out. When someone attacked Taobao with the issue of charging, he said, "When Taobao starts charging one day, let me announce the news to the public." Now he is working in the Taobao Mall department, but I don't know whether he announced the news of charging. The Mall was under another round of attack because of the issue of charging. I didn't know if it was planned by the same group of opponents (I was too imaginative to be responsible for the words above).

There was a technical detail in this project that was worth mentioning. Taobao Commodity Details Page had more than 1 billion views every day, the contents of which were stored in the cache. During the Good Fortune project, we needed to show the sellers the number of commodity views, which must be updated in real time while cache were generally updated asynchronously. So we added a field in the commodity table. As the field updated for each additional PV, an hour after publishing, the database could not handle so frequent updates and broke down. What could we do in this case? The normal caching strategy did not support real-time updating. Duolong worked out a way to write a module into Apache, allowing the number to be written into a centralized cache without going through the underlying Web container (only through Apache). Then the data in this cache would be asynchronously updated to the database. Any problems could always be easily solved in Duolong's hands.

A lot of things happened that year, too many for me to keep in mind. I could only vaguely remember that by the end of the project, there were some adjustments to the organizational structure of the team, and a lot of great people were recruited, especially UEDs, for example, Santong of XX (@XX的三通) (he and I were two of the four disciples of Yideng), Zhao Xiaoma (@赵小马), Yuning, Yuanxin, and others. At that time UEDswere divided into interaction design, user research, front-end, and other sectors, while all the work was undertaken by one or two people before. In that project, we had an in-depth cooperation. As the project PM, I felt that the project cycle was even longer after division of UED.

The miserable year passed slowly, but at the end of the year I was raised to the level of P6.

In the spring of 2007, my wife went to her parents' home to give birth to our baby while I tried to give birth to my baby in the company—the next project: Taobao Travel. The reason I considered this project as my own baby was because I was involved in it as early as the business survey. Back then, Alipay provided interfaces for a bunch of ticket agents and found a great profit margin and high level of electronization and standardization in this business. Though Alipay wanted to create a platform of travel services, their R&D personnel were all engaged in their own work. So they had no choice but to come to Taobao for cooperation. We worked out a group-version travel service package, which could either access Taobao and Alipay, or the B2B system. Our first version of Taobao Travel required the user to log into an Alipay account, which was almost the same as the user system of etao.com. To the surprise of many people, we did not use the user information of Taobao. My supervisors sent me to work with Alipay since I was at a loose ends at that time and familiar with the business of Alipay. So after an absence of two years, I once again collaborated with Alipay.

I went together with BD Sun Quan and Xia Bobo from Alipay to visit airlines for negotiations on ways of cooperation and a revenue sharing model. It was the first time I had sat at the negotiating table with such arrogant state-owned enterprises. The only thing that I needed to do was to provide technical analysis when they asked me whether something was achievable. In state-owned enterprises, there were many talented visionaries, who wanted to do something innovative, but were restricted by the system. After six months' fruitless negotiations, we had to turn to the ticket agents. These businessmen were very sensitive to the potential of this business, and they realized that this certainly would develop into a huge market, as the platform was open to all Taobao users. They were so active in the business that the Taobao Travel mode soon became a service platform for agents, who shared revenue with us after making money (you want to know how much we shared? I won't tell you).

After tough business negotiations, there were even more difficult project development follow-ups. Since my wife was not in Hangzhou in those days and had stopped asking me "Do you still love me," I devoted myself to the project. By the end of 2007, Taobao Travel was launched. When I asked my bosses what domain to use, Yuyan said that the plainest and easiest-to-remember one was the best. So jipiao.taobao.com won out. The first deal on this platform was a ticket booked by the owner of an agency for himself. As per the revenue sharing rules, we made a few bucks from that deal. That afternoon, Caishen and Yuyan came to our group with a crowd of colleagues from the Operations Department to send out gold coin chocolates as celebration of our first income. I was pushed around by a group of people and we took group photos all together, but no one gave me a copy later. In this project, Xiaoyu was PD, Yeqing, and Wenwan were responsible for operation support, and Yuning undertook the work of interaction design (from then on, I have developed profound friendships with more and more female colleagues. So I often joked about writing an anecdotal biography titled *12 Most Important Women in My Life*. LOL). Our development team included Zhenbei, Kongwang, Qingxu, and Tengyi (they are four of the *12 Most Important Men in My Life*. Ha!).

At that time, the first and second largest players in the domestic flight ticket market were Ctrip and eLong. Even after a long time since the launch of our platform, users were still used to calling them to book tickets. The pace of development of Taobao Travel was actually very slow. On the other hand, in order to obtain real-time flight information, we needed the support of TravelSky (AKA China TravelSky Holding Company), which was eager to promote their hotel system. So in the next six months, we developed Taobao Hotel on the basis of TravelSky's hotel system and integrated it into Taobao Travel, together with the ticketing system. TravelSky also provided the IBE (Internet Booking Engine) interface for us. Our operations department and I kept our eyes on the progress of ticket and hotel booking on our platform all day long. If someone's classmates, colleagues, relatives, or friends were going traveling, we would recommend Taobao Travel to them. I can still remember that we had only sold a few hundred tickets by the end of 2008.

The team next to our office was Taobao Lottery, whose PM was Zhebie and project manager was Yideng. After the "My Taobao AJAX Edition" incident, Yideng's technical level was greatly improved, and he talked a good game about AJAX and user experience when negotiating with lottery companies. This project enjoyed all the favorable advantages: users could buy a lottery ticket for only two yuan, and it was very convenient to buy a ticket with Alipay. Sales soared after the launch, and by the end of the year, two users had won the 5 million yuan prize, making it one of the most popular products at that time. However, we the miserable ticket team could only enviously watch them making a hit.

I watched my baby growing up slowly but steadily, during which we did a little work for occasional daily needs. At that time, another

group of people were locked up in the Lakeside Garden for Taobao Mall. When they came back from the Lakeside Garden, Taobao Travel was integrated into the Taobao Mall as a vertical market project, and our team was combined into the technical team of Taobao Mall. Every time I had a weekly meeting with Xingdian and other team members, I had nothing to share when they talked about Taobao Mall. By the end of the year, Taobao Mall grew vigorously, but the ticket business still had not seen much improvement. As my technical level did not have much progress, I only got a score of 3.25 by the end of year and was still rated as P6 level.

But for the first time, some companies tried to poach me.

The Fifth Year (2008–2009).

Some readers wonder if I would drop this series later. In fact, it gets harder and harder for me to write, because the people involved are right beside me, and I have to take into account their feelings. And the things I am writing just happened not long ago or are still in progress, which are difficult for me, a person involved, to offer an objective description. But since I have written so much, it would not hurt to go on. The things I am going to write about happened recently and were not well-known enough to attract the readers' interests.

Once I wrote a blog article about the "dark room." It is Taobao's tradition to have all important projects carried out in the dark room.

When we did My Taobao and Good Fortune projects, I was envied by other people for being locked up in the dark room. In 2008, I started to envy others who worked in the dark room.

There were two sets of people who had experienced the dark room: one group did the legendary Taobao Mall, and the other did the legendary Taobao System 3.0.Putting aside the group of Taobao Mall, the system of Taobao's main station experienced a tremendous change at that time.

Taobao's system had been in flux, as it developed too fast. But there were only two large scale version changes: one was migrating the initial system of LAMP architecture to the Java platform, and the other was splitting the centralized Java system into a multi-layer distributed system. Migration from PHP to Java was completed in 2004. When Sun's engineers were developing Alipay, I had just joined Taobao and missed this opportunity. When the centralized Java platform was split into a multi-layer distributed system, I was engaged in Taobao Travel, and missed it again.

I always believe that vertical markets like Taobao Travel are the best business model. It is not possible for all commodities to be displayed in the same way, nor is it impossible for all deals to use the same process. Before the main station was split, the vertical market required a brand new system, while after the split, it only needed to be restructured on the business logic layer. So this split not only shored up the rising flow, but also supported the development of new business of the subsequent years. There were many technological innovations in the process of splitting, meaning that we have already moved from the stage of using technology to the one of creating technology. I remember once when we communicated with Tencent's engineers, we mentioned the file storage system we developed based on GFS: Taobao built up the TFS (Taobao File System), and Tencent developed a TFS (Tencent File System) of their own—different innovation from the GFS theory. In addition, we also developed the Key-value caching system, messaging middleware, Java middleware, massive data storage and calculation. For a system of a billion page views, you have to make some technological innovation.

I had missed all of these.

But Taobao Travel experienced very slow development during the first two years, while Taobao Mall was doing business innovations and the main station was making technical innovations. Our team drifted outside Taobao Mall and the main station. Some head hunters contacted me again at that time, trying to poach me.

I always tend to be persuaded by women, especially beautiful women, and Guofu is a woman of this category. She asked me what challenges would the testing face after splitting of Taobao's main station. I said that the probability of error was larger with more system hierarchies, but functional tests could not detect the lower hierarchies.

She asked if there was a way to test down on the code level. I said yes, but very difficult. She said that was exactly why she came to me, and asked what method I would use. I said unit testing, but better to leave it to the engineers, and we only needed to test interfaces of the upper hierarchy. She said that great minds thought alike, and they already had some people working on it, and she asked if I wanted to be involved to further expand the project. Only then did I found out that she had dug a pit for me to jump in. However, this was a great change of Taobao's development. If I could get this straight, it might largely guarantee the stability of the system. Besides, I was a little tired of selling flight tickets every day, and wanted to do something that no one had ever tried.

I worked as a developer, PM, and part-time PD before, and also developed several process as an SQA. At the end of 2008, I began a career as a test engineer. In the test team, I realized that my previous knowledge about testing was too shallow. Particularly, Taobao's test team had state-of-the-art testing skills and methods in the industry. What I had to do was to recruit a team that could not only write Java code but also had appropriate ideas and approaches of testing. But later I found no such person, so I had to recruit people who could write codes and give them training on testing methods, or recruit people who could do testing and train them for code writing. During the first half of 2009, I put most of my energy into recruiting and training, resulting in an increase of team members from 4 to 19. When I was working on the training of interface testing engineers together with Tiehua, a colleague nicknamed Procuress gave us a name of "Flower and willow."

The idea of interface testing was very simple: use test codes to verify the correctness of system code logic. But it was easier said than done. The biggest problem was that the test code was too open to changes. It changed now and then and even failed often. Another problem was that a business logic might need 10 times more test codes to cover, which was both a lot of work and time-consuming. We discovered that lower system hierarchies had smaller changes and simpler logic. So we started testing from the bottom hierarchies of IC, TC, and UIC. Test codes were put into continuous integrated environment after being written. Once the code under testing submitted a SVN, the test code regressed once, and released the error messages. 2009 was an exceptionally difficult year for the team, as we did interface testing for all underlying codes, and performance testing for some. I do remember that we simulated over 1 billion requests during the UIC interface testing, and found a bug in JDK and submitted it to Sun Microsystems. During the process of testing, we also standardized the test method and developed a test framework in our book, called Interface Test White Paper.

I told Guofu that since we had achieved so much and had strong technical strength, we could keep high profile to spread our influence. So we proposed a vision: "Be the standard of the test industry." She designated us, the Flower and Willow combination, to maintain the blog (qa.taobao.com) and organize a large number of internal learning and training, which we call "3T Exchange" (Taobao Test Technology, Taobao Test Team or Taobao Test Training).

I had a lot of fun in the test team, and also had the opportunity to work together with more lovely girls. But from a lot of people's point of view, it was a bit strange for a developer to do testing. I often thought about whether it was good for me to shift between different posts. According to the popular dividing method of three types of youngsters on the Internet, I briefly divide engineers into the three categories: ordinary engineers who follow business requirements and do whatever they are asked to; artistic engineers who focus on their own areas and study in depth; and idiotic engineers who jump between different posts but only scratch the surface. There is an additional type of engineers, called geek engineers, who are competent and proficient at any job (referred to as a so-called "God" by us engineers). I think I belong to the third, but fortunately, there are so many opportunities in Taobao for me to do all the things I like.

By the end of 2008, my level was upgraded from P6 to M1. But the tragedy is that, a year later, the company paid more attention to professional competence, i.e. M1 = P6.

Probably because I did a good job of training in the test team, at the end of 2009, another company approached me again.

The Sixth Year (2009–2010)

As a ridiculous engineer, I gradually went off track. In 2009, I began to do little code-writing and had to deal with other miscellaneous things like coordination, resource allocation, and relationship management, which transformed me from a P to an M. (In a sense, I was no longer a code writer.) However, it was not until I became a manager that I came to realize management is really an art. Back then I learned a theory from a master hand that an M can never please everyone. So I believed, that for me, who tries to please everyone, management can't be an easy job. After two years as an M, someone said I was a nice, easy-going man, which was really a big blow on me, because it means I hadn't done a good job as an M.

At the end of 2009, a high-level supervisor sought me out from the recommendation of someone, as I learned later. I thought something serious was taking place, but it turned out that they needed a professional technical training team as the expanded employee group had great obstacles in expanding their knowledge base. I, who had done various things and often organized trainings and exchange events, seemed to be a suitable candidate. I think the growth of a team is the second priority (getting your job done is the first), and I can play a greater role by supporting the growth of a large team than simply managing a small one. But I had built the small team from scratch and recruited most of the people by browsing numerous CVs and making countless calls. Deeply attached to my team, I was very reluctant to forsake it. To leave or to stay? I had a serious internal conflict.. Thinking that the members of my team were all able to work on their own and my leaving would have no impact on them, I finally decided to leave, with tears in my eyes.

In this year of testing, it seemed that I was again thrown into the initial startup phase. Everything had to be done from scratch—theories, methods, skills, and the team. And I gradually became familiar with the members of the testing team. Together, we groped our way forward. This year, my technology and management levels didn't see much improvement. Instead, I made a number of mistakes—failing to identify the problems among team members, being simple and crude when handling issues related to staff relationships, and neglecting details when making arrangements. But after all this, my mind came to a different state. After the chaos, I calmed down.

Then our new team came into being. Zhan Tang (@展堂), Good Morning Vivian (@早安薇薇安), and Weird Greatness (@奇怪的伟大) were the first ones to join in. We gave our team a grand name—Taobao University of Technology (@ 淘宝技术大学). It was meant to be a corporate university, like HP Business School and Motorola University, but we didn't know exactly what to do. Considering that hundreds of fresh graduates were recruited into the company and many techniques couldn't be acquired outside, we decided to train them first.

So the first project of Taobao University of Technology was launched. We called it "Wave Riding Class" implying that the back waves ride on the front ones. We collected all the business cases, frameworks, specifications, procedures, and working methods, and imparted them to the newcomers. After all the knowledge was collected, we found it would take two months to complete the training. So, the earliest trainees of the Wave Riding Class received two months' training provided by us. Then we interviewed the trainees and found a big problem—the amount of knowledge was too much for most to absorb. . But some students were just as talented as Xuzhu and could assimilate the knowledge easily. They grew up quickly.

In 2010, we focused on the training of fresh graduates. The project of the Wave Riding Class experienced several modifications. We classified the knowledge and perfected the courses before the final version came into being: the fresh graduates received two weeks' off-the-job training about general skills provided by the Wave Riding Class; the advanced skills were classified for the on-the-job training which was called Wind Chasing Class; experience sharing and master exchange were called Lecture Room, and the three-day off-the-job training was called the Soaring Class which imparted Taobao's unique techniques and frameworks to the market-recruited employees. What supported these projects included a lecturer management system, a course management system, and an online registration platform.

In our work we conducted a number of innovations. A training manager of a brother company once gave such an account: they went to a training company to purchase a database course but the training company said, "The best DBAs are all in your company. How can I find them elsewhere?" Only then did we find that much of the top talent in the industry was actually inside our company.

So, could we purchase courses from internal lecturers as we did from outside? Having gained the supervisors' approval, we began to offer heavy rewards for such courses within the company. It takes at least 8 hours to thoroughly explain a certain technique. Therefore, an excellent course design and teaching abilities are needed. After the compensations were posted, a dozen such courses were brought forward. In fact the heavy compensations were still much lower than that which they could get for teaching outside. And the teaching that lasted at least a whole day was a lot of extra work. It felt right to give them additional rewards. So, after a few classes, we gave them each an iPad. Holding the iPads in their hands, they felt very proud, which also was great advertising for Taobao University of Technology.

In the process of the rapid development, our team expanded too. Tang Tian cr (@唐甜cr) and Wind Cloud Grin (@风云咧咧嘴) joined in. A few interns passed through, and the real name of one of them was registered as the account name of a class coordinator and finally became a nickname. In addition, I'd like to mention a brother team which has close relations with us. We do internal training while they do external training. So far, they have successfully held two sessions of @velocityChinaWeb performance, operation, and maintenance conference, as well as many exchange conferences on D2, iData, iTest, aDev, etc. They focus on the external side while we focused on the internal. The head of the team is Ling Xiaoshan (@灵小珊), a straightforward girl.

In 2009, I was just transferred from the testing department to the technology university. I wasn't promoted and I think I was indeed not qualified then. At the end of 2010, I was confident. Back then, Taobao changed its promotion system. You needed to give a report to a promotion committee. Many people were devastated after they

returned from the interviews, and I was one of them. The supervisors asked me one question: "What do you think is the essence of training?" I replied it was a good question. The result was that I remained at the rank of M1.

The Seventh Year (2010–2011)

This part begins with some advertisements. Enjoy!

First, I'd like to help Fat Hu Fei (@胖胡斐) market his new book *Things Are Different Now*, which tells how to run a store at Taobao successfully. One word can describe it: practical. It mentions the rules of lucky draw. In fact the code of one of the events was written by me exactly. And my name appears in the chapter "Charming Attributes" too.

My second advertisement is for the Chinese version of *Tapworthy: Designing Great iPhone Apps*, translated by Bao Zongxi. The excellent book focuses on user interactions of iPhone Apps. I've met plenty of talented people in Taobao, but Fat Hu Fei and Bao are among the few who won my total worship. Fat Hu Fei and I used to learn driving together. When backing a car, we usually looked back to see the rear. But Fat Hu Fei was too fat to do this. He had to look at the rear view mirror while going in reverse. Also, he always went beyond the edge when driving around a circle. The jokes made by Hua Li / Zeng Xianjie (@华黎曾宪杰) and the coach almost drove him mad. I admire Zongxi because he can always achieve something out of whatever he does. Zongxi has a great knowledge of photography and the OM19's Time initiated by Zongxi has brought out a good number of photography fans. He's no longer in Taobao, but the organization is still running.

The last advertisement is for our team. In the first year, we merely felt our way forward with the Taobao Technology College, having trained hundreds of fresh graduates. The second year, 2011, saw the golden age of our college. First, I'd like to introduce our team members: Zhan Tang (@展堂), Good Morning Vivian (@早安薇薇安), Tang Tian cr (@ 唐甜cr), Weird Greatness (@ 奇怪的伟大), Wind Cloud Grin (@风云咧咧嘴), DY-Duan Yan (@ DY - 段燕), Gao Xiaogao (@高小糕), Ciera Mi_Mi (@ Ciera 米 _ 米), and some others who didn't have a Weibo account.)

In 2011, our team expanded and we could do more things. After a demand survey was made in early 2011, we developed a series of courses targeting core systems and fundamental products, including cloud computing series, mass storage series, Oracle series, MySQL series, operating system series, minority language series, JVM series, Java memory optimization, search technology series, and advertising technology series. Some other courses have also been developed based on the key words of the company's technology strategy in recent years—stability, performance, cost, and user experience—including the stability series, performance optimization series, and user experience series. Based on the common popular techniques, we developed the courses of seckilling system design and optimization, and the technology system behind the Double 11 Shopping Festival. We have brought forth a technology feast.

Here I'd like to say that my admiration for the leaders of our company has been growing with the rapid development of Taobao's technology team in the recent years. The Technology Committee was established to guide technical development and carry out talent evaluation; teams dedicated to performance, stability, cost, and user experience were also established; highly capable professionals were employed to deal with significant indexes. The whole network system went forward on a sound track. In recent years, Taobao's technology has been more and more open; an open platform for developers was set up; our core structure and middleware were made open too; even our hardware structure of low-consumption servers were made open-sourced. Previously Taobao had obtained some techniques from the open source community, and now it's time for us to sincerely give back to the entire Internet.

At the same time, we reached forward. Together with the company's HR, we went to campuses. We established Taobao Clubs in Zhejiang University and Dalian University of Technology, bringing several great courses and experimental projects to the students. Also, together with the Group and ACM China Committee, we held a summer forum and a qualifying competition, offering a good chance for the students to know about our enterprise and for our R&D department to know about the excellent students.

In the first half of 2011, I was still racking my brains on such issues as the essence of training. Thinking about it, I didn't do much. It was the women in the group who were working hard. With their great power, they organized over 400 training sessions; even the supporting lecturers for feedback totaled more than 300; each engineer of our R&D department was offered almost 14 hours of training. I learned from the ASTD International Conference & Exposition 2009 Report that the training hours per person total 19 hours or so in US. enterprises with great training programs, while the average time is only less than 5 hours in the recorded Chinese enterprises with training programs. However, the per capita output of our training administrators exceeded the US. data in 2009.

When I was talking about concepts and data, the staff was already working on the details — how to arrange the desks and chairs to make the arrangement more reasonable, how to invite trainees to have a higher attendance, what problems lecturers tended to meet in classes, how big the words on PPT should be to allow the back-row trainees to see clearly, and more They divided the training process into detailed steps, making an operation guide for each step. Gradually they accumulated a lot of knowledge and experience.

So what on earth is the essence of training? Inspired by our supervisor, we concluded that the essence of training is a circulation of knowledge which aims to promote the growth of employees and eventually business improvement. And some supervisors may ask, "How do you prove that you have played a role in enhancing the company's business?" That's a good question. Well, one day I heard an advertisement for Nongfu Spring Water which said: "We don't produce water; we're only the carriers for nature." Then I was inspired. "We don't produce knowledge; we're only the carriers of knowledge." The more we carry, the more people will receive, and the higher our value will be. I don't know if my bottle of knowledge has saved a thirsty life or made someone choke. What I'm sure of is that it must be valuable somehow.

Thanks to the team effort, I was promoted to M2 in a special promotion event held in the middle of the year.

Mr. Ma once said, "What never changes is change itself." After the promotion event, the company underwent a radical change. Taobao was divided into four units—Taobao.com, etao.com, Tmall.com, and Shared Business Platform. And I belonged to Shared Business Platform. Later the Platform was divided and I became a part of the Group. Those who had changed together with us included the newly-established Product College and Operation College. Naturally the three academies were united to become the Taobao Academy. The former principal became president of the academy and I became principal of the Technology College. A larger staff team allowed us to combine our resources to do something big, but the management group needn't be so large. Besides, what I do can be categorized either into P or into M. But a nice "M" probably wouldn't have a promising future. So I transferred myself to be P7 with the title of Training Expert in the category of Experts and Professors.

Seven years have passed, and my hair has grown thinner. I devoted 7 years of my youth to Taobao and I've gained a lot, like money. Apart from that, the most valuable things include getting to know a bunch of talented people, making some friends, and having an experience I can boast about.

The Eighth Year (2011–2012)

The first snowfall in Hangzhou of the year on January 3, 2013 came a little earlier than usual. The snow kept falling down throughout the day, and I had known that I couldn't drive to work the next morning. I had intended to take a bus this morning, but there were so many people that I just couldn't get on the bus after waiting for half an hour. Therefore, I decided to walk to the company despite the 8-kilometer journey ahead. However, after walking through 2 kilometers, I was exhausted and went into a Starbucks nearby. My boss asked us online to write a review of the year 2012, so I turned on my computer, and I am now starting to write.

The year of 2012 was full of changes. You could never expect what you were going to do in the next quarter in Alibaba. In 2011, Taobao was divided into four parts: Taobao, Tmall, eTao, and Juhuasuan. I then became a member of Alibaba Group and moved from the Operations Department to the HR Department. In early 2012, CEO Jack Ma put forward the concept of "One Company," which means sharing resources in the group, promoting work transfer of leaders and promoting service integration. Due to the implementation of this concept, I had a new superior whose new superior was the vice president in charge of HR issues. However, soon after the superior had taken up the position and invited us to dinner, we got another new superior. He was a man who had his own plans. Unlike other newly assigned superiors who were eager to prove their ability, he did nothing to prove himself for three months, but invited us to dinners and observed how we did our work.

In fact, we were constantly seeking progress under such circumstances. The Technology University, the Operation University and the Product University had been lately combined, and we often exchanged views on the creation of a learning pattern. We believed that the off-line training was our primary product. It posed two problems. First, as the company expanded and more offices were set up in various regions, the cost of offline training would be increased. Besides, it took great courage to walk one thousand meters to another building under the scorching sun of July and August to attend a class. Another problem was that training for different services varied. With services separating from or combining with each other, the offline training which was unified at the group-level could not meet the demand of members of small groups for learning about their own services.

What should the product 2.0 look like? We believed that it should be a product for online learning, which was easier said than done. Online learning generally has four patterns: playing videos, reading documents, live broadcasts, and FAQs. To make a video, one should pay attention to the video's definition and the clarity of sound. Videos shot in an ordinary classroom usually feature over-bright screens, shadowy figures, and background noises of car horns and birds' tweeting. In addition, one has to adjust the focal length when he takes a scene of a lecturer writing something on a white board. Therefore, such video production is quite demanding in terms of equipment, environment, and a cameraman's proficiency. To make good videos, we cooperated with *Tao*, which is the official media production of the Alibaba Group, borrowing their equipment and acquiring their shooting techniques. At present, we are able to make videos which are a little better than those shot with a family DV camera. In terms of online documents, it was more difficult to make their content attractive to readers than to produce the content, because we could not present too much substantial content in PPT or produce PDF files of a long length which few people would like to read. We cooperated with Taohua in live broadcast. We adopted online Flash technologies which were relatively more developed but were still subject to hardware-related factors like video camera and classroom environment. We acquired the question-and-answer model from Zhihu (which is a Chinese question-and-answer website where questions are created, answered, edited, and organized by the community of its users), and in this model, students could create a learning community by asking questions and inviting colleagues to answer these questions. The difficulty of running such a model lies in the fostering of early users and the promotion of high quality content.

Despite the many difficulties, we started to work on the online learning program after unanimous approval. The administrator of the program devoted considerable effort to learning the use of professional video cameras and editing videos. Within half a year in 2012, we uploaded videos of more than 30 courses (it took generally two days to shoot and edit a video). In terms of the online documents, there was a person in the Group who was extremely enthusiastic about knowledge management and uploaded several thousand documents. The live video broadcast was a pilot one. We opened live broadcast channels for staff to watch some key courses online, including those about the latest research of Zhengxiang, Bixuan, and Chuba. The

FAQs channel was operated by the group Problem Girls and presented a lot of high-quality content, including a module named "Yuan Fang, what do you think?", and this contributed a lot to the creation of a great atmosphere of the learning community.

It is a long process to explore these new learning patterns. We can easily establish a platform and upload something onto the platform, but the most important thing is that we must constantly maintain the content of the platform and promptly update information. As I believe, only by keeping our enthusiasm and continuing to put great effort to the development of the online learning platform will the platform play a greater role than offline training.

I would like to say something about knowledge management here. I do somehow disagree with this concept, because knowledge can be managed in traditional industries, but not in the Internet industry. Knowledge in the Internet industry is updated frequently, and it will have been outdated when you start to manage it. I think that we don't need to manage such knowledge; instead, we should externalize tacit knowledge and diffuse such knowledge as soon as possible within its life cycle. We don't need to wait for the knowledge to be accumulated; on the contrary, we should allow the free flow of knowledge, which can create great value.

My superior discussed new learning patterns with us, and also followed the philosophy of the "One Company" concept, promoting the sharing of training services within the Group. The three universities in our group originally belonged to Taobao.com, and there were Century Technology Universities in B2B and Alipay. The Technology University provided on-the-job training as well as training for freshly-minted graduates. Different universities had private communications with each other, but they had never shared resources or used a shared platform. In short, they were operated separately. To implement the One Company concept, we launched the Three Lower-Level Shares project and the Three Higher-Level Shares project. The "Three Lower-Level Shares project was meant to share training resources, including courses, lecturers, and solutions; while the Three Higher-Level Shares project was meant to use a shared training platform with all training resources being presented on the platform. I was Project Manager of the Three Lower-Level Shares project and Susu (Su Jie, author of *Everyone is a Product Manager*) was Project Manager of the other.

At the beginning of summer in 2012, the training staff on both sides of the Qiantang River who engaged in B2B, Alipay, and Taobao started to carry out the Three Shares project. We had so many meetings that I just couldn't remember the exact number. However, changes came when we nearly finished the work. On June 20, 2012, B2B was delisted and divided into CBU and ICBU, and the Technology University of the original B2B was combined with the Group. Henceforth, we became a unity in the sense of organization structure.

After we became a unity, there came a hot summer when we set out another large project: recruitment. I helped those who were in charge of the recruitment with the examination of drafts of speeches for campus recruitment. In the meantime, I took over a project with an exotic name of Ivy Plan. The main philosophy of the project was that we would only recruit the best students and train them as elite technicians. The question was how to train these students. We had never received any formal training and were entirely free to develop ourselves. We would like to know if there were some shared features among us. Therefore, we visited some people who had made quick progress and asked them as well as their superiors and colleagues relevant questions, whereby we could figure out their growth pattern and devise training plans for new employees accordingly. The above-mentioned is some general information about the Ivy Plan, and I won't go into any further details because it may involve some confidential information.

It was already the autumn of 2012 when we worked out the Ivy Plan, and I began to work with a lady who was in charge of the Group's innovation project called Horse Racing (in which staff could put forward their ideas about some innovative projects and implement these projects if the projects were approved by the Group). She was responsible for the overall arrangements of the project while I worked as her assistant and occasionally acted as a judge. I contributed a little to the technological innovation and service innovation of the Group in this way. I had some thoughts after having participated in the project for three months: both external and internal innovations suffered from much stress. It was useless if someone only had some ideas but not presented real products; and sometimes, it was not enough to only present the products, and the products must be able to be launched onto the market immediately. What's more, internal innovations were threatened by plagiarism and faced competitions from "official" products.

After writing so much, I have found that I was only a participant or a supporter in the above-mentioned matters. What I have done in 2012 is hard to classify, and in most cases, things could be accomplished with other people being the main strength of a group. Yet I made some unexpected by products in supporting the implementation of these things. For example, to support the development of the FAQs channel, I had been browsing zhihu.com (the Chinese question-and-answer website,) for some time and answered some questions on the website, and I unexpectedly "became one of those whose answers can receive at least one thousand "likes" and was listed among the Top 250 Users" (this is the comment from Huang Jixin, co-founder of Zhihu). I also sorted out materials about the technology development of Taobao over the past few years, and they were recommended by the Sina.com blog as headlines in the IT section. Moreover, many publishers contacted me, hoping to have them published.

In the last month of 2012, I had been asking myself how much I could still contribute to the development of technicians. The answer was a little disappointing, because I had been away from the forefront of work for three years and had sorted out all the technologies that I

knew and shared them with my colleagues. In terms of the exploration of the learning patterns, we have made some achievements, and my colleagues will go further into the issue. If I were a piece of firewood with one end being the learning pattern, I could have burnt this end to ashes and then, I could turn around and burn the other end. I have missed the development of cloud computing and big data, and have not been engaged in the operation of Taobao for a long time. Therefore, I want to make up what I have missed. Feiqing, who is vice president of Tmall and takes charge of Jushita, found me when I was thinking about this issue. Haha, I can get everything I want in Jushita.

Today should have been my first day in Jushita. However, the heavy snow has unexpectedly confined me to Starbucks. In this situation, I might as well look back upon what I have done in the past year and look to the future with my computer.

CHAPTER 7

Collective Biographies of 'Great Ps'

In the preceding chapters, we have already talked about how technology and business supplement each other and achieve a mutual development. There is a similar relationship between an enterprise and an individual: without a suitable platform, it would be difficult for a man with of good professional caliber to show his value; without suitable talent, even a robust enterprise is likely to see a bleak future. Fortunately, a large number of professionals have emerged in the vigorous development of Taobao, and Taobao also has enabled them to realize their value. Let's take a look at these people and their stories.

- **Zhengming—Senior Researcher of the Group's Core System**
- **Zhengxiang—Senior Researcher of Taobao, Head of the OceanBase Program**
- **Bixuan—Veteran Technical Expert of the Group's Core System**
- **Fangweng—Head of the Taobao Open Platform Program**
- **Wu Hanqing—Senior Security Expert of the Information Security Center of Aliyun**
- **Yunzheng—Veteran Technical Expert of Data Platform and Product Department**
- **Xiaoma—Senior Technical Expert of Taobao UED Front End Common Platform**
- **The Program World of Taobao's Legendary Engineer—Duolong**

Zhengming—Senior Researcher of the Group's Core System

Zhengming, senior researcher, is the person in charge of the Group's Core System. He was Chairman of "Great Taobao Technology Committee" in 2012. He graduated from National University of Defense Technology (NUDT) as a Computer Major with a doctorate in Engineering. He once worked as a chief scientist for TelTel, associate professor of NUDT, a kernel developer of RedHat, founder of LVS OSS, and co-founder of ChinaCluster.

Ziliu: Let me first congratulate you for being selected as Chairman of this year's (2012) "Great Taobao Technology Committee." It has been 3 years since the inception of the Technology Committee. At the annual meeting, there were some voices of doubt. For instance, the Technology Committee is a virtual organization without any power to mobilize resources and therefore, it is hard for the Committee to lead technology innovation apart from the work. As chairman of this year, what is your insight into these issues?

Zhengming: It has been two years since the establishment of the Committee. The Committee has played an active role in events including the compiling of Job Model, Promotion Assessment, Technology Race and Taobao Open Source. As you can see, our Committee has actually done something. Maybe we did not do enough promotion. Someone said that he went to the directors last year with an idea that was not so much relevant to the business and came back without obtaining any resource support. In fact, the program of Taobao Labs" in the Technology Race was not something done by

Wufeng alone, but the result of cross-team work. When he looked for resources, the Committee offered some help and his program was supported by Feiqing who allowed the people outside Taobao to join in the program and ensured the implementation of Taobao Labs. Actually, the Technology Committee is an additional channel apart from the business line where you can talk about your ideas and get the resources. Maybe we have not done enough promotion and many junior technical staff have no idea about it. We are going to make more coverage in promotion, including the influence that the Committee has among the junior staff, for example, the roles it plays and the functions it provides.

Ziliu: The technical team was divided into several parts last year, but technology should still be an organic whole. In the context of Great Taobao, what role does "Great Taobao Technology Committee" play? What will it bring to Taobao as a whole?

Zhengming: The different divisions in the framework of the company is consistent with business needs. The Technology Committee serves as a bond that links up the technology teams in each department. It is an organization of technical staff which shoulders no responsibility of business but features functions of interactions and learning. It will help the technical staff of Great Taobao make joint efforts and drive the development of Taobao technology in turn.

Ziliu: As new chairman of the Committee, what could you share with us about the technical planning of the Committee for the year to come?

Zhengming: Instead of a plan made from top to bottom, the planning involves all divisions of the Committee which make their plans separately per their own development. At present, there are altogether 7 divisions with a Wireless Division to be added in the future. As the planning is mainly made by the divisions, plans will be more vigorous if worked out in a bottom-to-top manner. As members of the standing committee, our main duty is to apply for more resources and set up a better incentive mechanism that allows the divisions to implement their work more freely and spontaneously with more innovative ideas. On the general technical assembly, we also plan to set up a platform for internal and external communications, for example, the Technology Committee Open Day, and we will build up a website of the Committee for internal communication (e.g. the Kongxianghui). With each of the divisions having its own development fund, Technology Committee is also going to set some awards to encourage programs like Technology Race and Technology Innovation. For external events, we will continue to support activities including Technology Carnival, Technology Salon, Velocity.

Ziliu: You have very rich technical experience. You developed the LVS system when you were a postgraduate and then conducted teaching at NUDT and later you started a business of your own and at last, you joined Taobao. Would you share with us the experience you had all along?

Zhengming: I did LVS when I was pursuing my doctorate. I started teaching at NUDT in 2000 and quit the job in 2006. I worked for my own for a while and joined in Taobao two years ago.

I worked on the LVS program in 1998. By 1999, there had been quite a few applications based on the program. At that time, a classmate of mine was in Shanghai where Fudan University was initiating a Start-up Competition for MBAs. He asked me if I had any idea. I described the LVS program to him and he participated in the competition but it seemed he didn't win any prize. Later, since we had already finished the business plan, we turned to some of our friends to see if we could get some investment, as the plan did appear promising. At the beginning of 2000, we had a seed fund. I was still dealing with my teaching at school at that time. And we founded a company. As it was during the Internet bubble period and we had no experience, we spent all that we had, about several million. This is how we started up. In fact, there is so much to consider in the start-up phase, including, the operation of the company, cash flow, market promotion, and so on.

Ziliu: How was the scale then?

Zhengming: There were up to 40 people at its peak time, with our offices based in Beijing and Shanghai.

Ziliu: What kind of program was it?)

Zhengming: The name of our website was chinacluster.com, i.e. China Cluster Corporation, a company that provided land balancing equipment and technology services based on LVS.

After a year or so, our company was shut down. I was still teaching in the university and doing research. I got married in 2001 and in 2002 my wife got her doctorate and wanted to go to Beijing. With her parents working for NUDT, she had been unable to travel afar from her kindergarten until she got her degree and she was so eager to leave this place after graduation. I happened to have a friend working at the Institute of Software Chinese Academy of Sciences (ISCAS). Our school sent me to work on a program with them, so we went to Beijing. At that time, what we saw in terms of the development of computer industry was MainFrame + dumb terminal, but now, it is the world of PC. This means intelligence has moved from the center to the margins and led to the generation of a new industry pattern. As for the communications industry, at that time, the whole system was in the hands of the operator, with the terminal only serving to receive and send messages. We predicted that intelligence in the communication industry would also move to the margins while the network would be supposed to be a “silly web” in charge of message receiving and sending. (However, for the present, the operator is still in strict control of that part.) A researcher in AT&T had researched the intelligent network for more than a decade, but later his theory was subverted by himself. He thought that intelligence should not be in the center, and it was even not right to study “intelligent networks.”. According to him, intelligence should be at the terminals. I read his research and seconded his idea. What he pointed out was just the opposite of the research of Bell Labs. He was dismissed later. But in my opinion, this was an inevitable trend. If we followed the trend and didn’t have too great expectations, we would succeed. We started our research based on our prediction. SIP protocol actually solved the communication problem between two Peers, through which the two Peers were able to find each other with one Session. As the protocol shared the same conception with us, we focused on SIP. However, the fact is that there were many household network gateways, which belonged to private IP addresses that required NAT address translation in order for the public network to be available. SIP protocol was a seven-layered protocol where no private IP was considered. With two peers both in private network, how could they find each other? NAT traverse was another problem at that time. An American company, Jasomi was able to solve this problem at the moment. One Jasomi machine was sold for tens of thousand of US dollars. It was really extortionate. I looked at their specifications and found it was not very difficult to do. It happened to be the time when SARS broke out in Beijing and I was staying at home, with nothing to do. Therefore, I finished writing the program with this function. Not disturbed by anyone else, I was highly efficient with my work. Later, we found Cathay Networks, a small company specializing in SIP Proxy, in Silicon Valley with the help of Cisco. The company was also running out of money. So we worked together. Then we had SIP-related technologies and had no idea of what to do with it.

One of the applications we did was Meet2talk which provided users with the function of chatting, similar to voice chatroom or conference call. The application was oriented toward terminal users instead of enterprises. But it was not popular among the common public since we did not intend to make it entertaining. So the number of users was small. Later, we wanted to develop voice chatting software oriented to acquaintances. We did TelTel in 2004, after the promotion of which, we found that there was already Skype in the market, which was released in September 2003. We also found some technical problems that led to breakdowns when faced with large scale users. In addition, some of the colleagues in the USA wanted to leave and the program was no longer able to carry on. I was doing NAT traverse support for them in China and doing other programs at the same time. At the end of 2003, we did a program called bitcool.tv in China which allowed the users to upload some MP3, videos, and Flash for playing and downloading. We failed to see the great value of Flash technology. Neither did we know the value of traffic. Many multimedia files were played in the source format which required a lot of traffic and great cost on bandwidth. As we could not afford the money of traffic, we promoted a P2P client application aBitCool. We received a lawyer's letter from Hollywood as there were copyright issues.

Ziliu: So close to working out a YouTube?

Zhengming: We were so close, if we had held on…(Laughter)

As the colleagues in the USA were leaving, we had to take over the R&D of voice communication there. We solved the problem of providing support for a large number of users, but we found it difficult to make a profit through this application. PC users were accustomed to using the applications for free while telephone communication was in the charge of the operators (even now Skype hasn't made a fortune); therefore we didn't have pricing power. We had some investment from D-Link. The company had a lot of network equipment but the users did not know how to use them. With our SIP technology, we could have access to the information. We cooperated with D-Link, and worked out products such as SIP Phone, SIP Camera, and SIP Digital Photo Frame. However, these were niche products and did not sell well. Later, we found Internet TV quite promising and we made a 9X9.TV (cloud TV) which allowed the users to organize their own TV programs and create a TV station of their own or subscribe to others' programs. They could download the content with our equipment and play them on their TV set. With SARFT's ban that no content on the Internet is allowed to be brought to TV, it was hard for us to carry on the program at home.

Ziliu: It has been over two years since you joined Taobao. At first, you focused on large-scale promotion of LVS and HAproxy, and then the optimization of the CDN system and you have launched the program of GreenCompute. Would you introduce the overall work planning for these years?

Zhengming: The planning for these years is to create a fundamental platform of high performance, extensibility, availability, and low cost for Taobao.com. Our main job is to make continuous optimization on these four dimensions. At the beginning, the CDN that Taobao adopted was Citrix NetScaler for commercial use, which was the best load balancer in the industry. However, as the scale of Taobao grew larger and larger, the requests to load small pictures increased a lot, which caused a lot of problems to Citrix. The traffic of a 10 G network card was 3 GB/s at most. Once it exceeded 3 GB/s, and up to 4 GB/s, the system would break down. In the CDN system, the processing of pictures was the greatest challenge. Compared to continuous data like videos, this kind of data with a smaller size and dispersed format was a high demand for access to hard disks. From the end of 2008 to the early 2009, what Taobao used was solely the SSD format, which meant higher cost for each CDN node, around RMB 2 million without load balancer included. Moreover, the traffic of one Netscaler was 3 GB/s at most, with 6 GB/s for two. And we didn't apply heartbeat line between the two NetScalers though it supported this function, as we were afraid that once either of the two NetScalers was broken, the traffic of 6 GB/s would be transferred to the other and the result would be devastating. And this is the problem with the commercial system: it is not suitable for special loading situations.

Then we started to modify gradually. We tried LVS+HAproxy. With advanced configuration, there was no problem to run at 100GB/s at one node. As to the cost, it was certainly impossible to spend recklessly on the back-end. So we started to use mixed storage, with SATA, SAS, and SSD being included. After the optimization, the effect was similar to that of a whole SSD and the storage was even larger and cache hit-rate higher. Currently, some of the best cache hit-rates are as high as 98%. Now the cost of a CDN node of the lowest standard with its traffic at 10 GB/s is reduced to RMB 500,000 and if it is low powered, the cost can be further reduced to RMB 370,000. We will continue improving it since there is no end in optimization.

What we pursue is better user experience, shorter response time, and lower cost at the same time.

Response time is the most concerning indicator, as it directly influences the user experience. In fact, Taobao has so far done a good job in terms of pictures optimization. For instance, during this year's Double 11 sale, the highest picture traffic we had was 856 GB/s, which might also be a record high worldwide. Now when you open a page on Taobao, the loading speed of a picture is very fast. The average response time for visiting pictures is 10ms or so but we will still work on it to see if it can be reduced to 9ms or 8ms, or even shorter. Though it will be much harder to improve on this, it is what we should do.

On the other hand, network transmission has always had a bottleneck. When there was a request for picture viewing, the processing time of the hard disk was 10ms, but in terms of network transmission, another 20ms might be needed, even when CDN was proper deployed. If there was a network problem, it could be extended to 70ms to 80ms. Therefore, there probably is greater potential to explore in the optimization of network protocol.

At the end of 2009, we decided to do a low-power program and we started with the CDN system over which we had good control. Since CDN has a relatively lower demand on data security—as it is all cache there anyway, it doesn't matter if the data was lost, and the global system could always cut off the bad nodes with little influence on the users—the low-power server was specially made to suit the CDN application. We undertook a lot during this period, and although it didn't go without hitches, we finally did it. We would like to thank many factories which were part of the program, including Viatech, Intel and Chaowei. In short, at last we were still able to run the server based on Atom and the effect of performance optimization has been the best so far, compared with other Intel processors. Actually a low-power server is just a small part of the entire green computing. The server consists of a high-performance server, apart from which, the network equipment, the rack, DC power supply, and the design of the whole data center all are green computing. Now we are customizing an Atom D525. In addition, there are also many types of low-power servers. So, what we do now is just a small part of the entire system. We share it with everyone, hoping others can join us, especially those Internet companies that also pay attention to the green data center. If everyone participates in this, it will greatly help drive the industry. We are now contacting colleagues in the industries, and the program is underway.

Ziliu: What made you join Taobao?

Zhengming: The past few years were rather a weary time for me, as I kept trying new ideas. However, the commercial outcomes could hardly meet our expectations. Sometimes you have good technologies, but it doesn't mean that you can find your customers, which makes it difficult to create any social values. But the social value of Taobao is apparent with its scale and challenges from its system so the technology will be able to bring value to the users very soon. I attended an Internet Hero Conference held in Hangzhou in 2007, after which, I was frequently approached by those who also attended the conference. After I finished my program at that time and rested for a while at home, I came and joined Taobao.

Ziliu: What do you predict will be some of the challenges that Taobao's systems might face?

Zhengming: The challenge in scale will become even more acute in the future. When the scale is expanded, the storage system for data, middleware, and the storage system for CDN will all need reconsideration. Now CDN has reached 1000 GB/s. When it reaches 3000 GB/s or even higher, we will have to consider the following aspects, including how to lower down the cost of bandwidth, if we need to build CND nodes with different scales, and if there should be hierarchical relations between them, taking the users experience into consideration at the same time. If our Hadoop cluster reaches 10,000, how shall we deal with the data layer at the back-end? We have to reconsider many issues of this kind.

Ziliu: You have been active in the open source community. What do you think we have gained from the community and what we have contributed to it?

Zhengming: We have gained considerable help from the open source community. For example, last year, we wished to improve the performance of the database. The decisive factor of the database is the I/O speed of memory. In the summer of 2010, Chuba and we focused on NVM products, i.e. those products that won't have the data lost when the power is cut-off. We contacted two Flash Memory manufacturers abroad specializing in PCI-E and tested for six months and the results turned out to be very satisfactory. Fuwei's team took away the IBM mini-computer in IC and replaced it with a high-end PC server. We helped replace the memory with a PC server plus PCI-E memory and optimized the database in five or six aspects, from the storage engine of innoDB to the I/O scheduler and Flash Cache and the optimization of file system. So we replaced Oracle, took away EMC storage and they worked well on IC. When it comes to TC, we replaced IOE (IBM minicomputer, Oracle, and EMC storage) in just one step. In 2010, there were only 2,000 transactions every second and the original target for 2011 was 5,000. But with PC server and PCI-E memory, a single server could support 10,000 transactions per second. The original solutions cost us RMB 20 million and now we just need RMB 120,000 for one server. For the sake of security, we used a 16X2 cluster, which cost only RMB 4 million. When TDDL layers are split up, the database alone can deal with 160,000 transactions per second, which means it will provide support for the development of Taobao in many years to come. The successful deletion of IOE marks a milestone for Taobao. The very core system of us has gotten rid of commercial software and depended wholly on open source software and a software system that sd developed. Therefore, I'd say the open source software means a lot to us.

Now we also make some of our software as open source so as to give back to the society, including TFS, Tair, WebX, and TEngine. We have more than one hundred open source programs on our Taocode platform, many of which are contributed by the engineers other than from Taobao. I believe the open source environment in China will get better.

Ziliu: What kind of suggestions would you like to offer those fledgling technicians?

Zhengming: Find what you are really interested in and invest your time in it. The expertise you have collected after practice is far more useful than what you get from the books. I once read a book on operation systems in English, where a Chinese saying was quoted, "I hear and I forget. I see and I remember. I do and I understand." This sentence has impressed me deeply. It was from the ancient Chinese philosopher Xunzi.

Ziliu: You have always been busy at work. But I also see pictures of your daily life on your Weibo. Would you describe something about your leisure time?

Zhengming: I just spend time with my kid. I love children. However, I am not the person who is charge of the family affairs. My job is mainly about playing with my child. Laugh.

Ziliu: Thanks Zhengming, for doing our interview and taking time out from your busy schedule. We may conclude Zhengming's story as "a life driven by technologies." Zhengming has blended technology into his blood.

Zhengxiang—Senior Researcher of Taobao, Head of the OceanBase Program

Having been a person with a lot of admiring titles, he, without a subordinate, is now devoted to a career admired by people with great awe, while he jokingly calls himself "a person with no taste". Now let's get to know this master of technology—Zhengxiang.

Dr. Yang Zhenkun, with a nickname of Zhengxiang in Taobao, is an honorary member of the Young Computer Scientists & Engineers Forum (YOCSEF) of China Computer Federation. Admitted into Peking University in 1984, he finished his undergraduate degree in only three years and postgraduate studies in more than one year and began to study for a doctorate under Wang Xuan at the tender age of 24. He was exceptional in being promoted to a professorship at such a young age in 1997 and was among the first batch of the specially employed professors of the Yangtze River Scholar Award at Peking University in 1999. He was awarded the First Class Award of Beijing Science and Technology Progress Award and of National Science and Technology Progress Award (ranking fourth), the 6th China Youth Science and Technology Award, Beijing Youth May Fourth Award, and other prizes. Having successively served as Vice President of the Founder Research Institute, Deputy Director of the Institute of Computer Science & Technology of Peking University, principal research fellow of Lenovo Corporate Research, chief research fellow of Microsoft Research, a senior scientist at Baidu, and is currently a senior research fellow at Taobao.

Such titles are enough to make him all-powerful across the circle and are likely to conjure up in your mind an image of a high-flyer or a mentor for life. However, the moment you see him, that image will be totally reversed by his sneakers, loose casual pants, shirt slightly out of shape and employee's card hung slantwise. Thin and tall, with clear and quiet eyes, he is always wearing a humble smile. This is Zhengxiang, AKA Yang Zhenkun. Many people are deeply impressed by his sartorial style and admire his casual and elegant manner, but he himself just hopes that others won't follow him in this respect for it is only a demonstration of his "lack of taste."

Others look at this master "without taste" in awe of his career, and he has succeeded in leading the research and development of Founder's sixth- and seventh-generation RIP (Raster Image Processor), making an irreplaceable contribution to the press and publication industry of China. Professor Wang Xuan, an academician of Chinese Academy of Sciences and President of Peking University Founder Research Institute, once praised him, "Yang Zhenkun created the first page description language interpreter of China, making a critical contribution in such aspects as the overall design, software structure and key algorithm of the new-generation RIP." Currently, he is presiding over the research and development of a big database, OceanBase, (oceanbase.taobao.org). The data of Taobao has far exceeded the largest scale which can be supported by a single relational database, and is growing rapidly. For Taobao, the research and development of OceanBase is not solely for the sake of saving costs; for without such technologies, it is impossible for Taobao to maintain its operation, given the number of computer rooms and costs.

How is Zhengxiang's study of such globally difficult issues going on? What legendary experiences can we find in such a computer whiz? What suggestions will he make for young people? What gossipy information can we find about him?

In order to figure out such questions, I had an interview with him. There was an interesting and noticeable act of Zhengxiang at the beginning of the interview. He went up the drinking fountain, with an empty mineral water bottle in hand, collected some water and put it at his foot.

Ziliu: Congratulations. The OceanBase program led by you was just given an award by the CJK OSS Award of this session. From your perspective, what's the significance of this prize?

Zhengxiang: This is a meeting (the 10th Northeast Asia OSS Promotion Forum) for the promotion of OSS which is jointly organized by the national department in charge of the information technology industry in China, Japan, and Korea, and the award is "the Sixth CJK OSS Technology Winning Award." Totally China has three pieces of software which won the award, all of which are produced by private enterprises; and OceanBase developed by Taobao ranked first.

Ziliu: What problem is OceanBase mainly intended to solve?

Zhengxiang: Relational databases had a mature theory in the 1960s and 1970s and its technologies and products became mature in the 1970s and 1980s, but its technology and theories have not made any great breakthroughs since then. However,demand is always changing and the scale of data today has posed a serious challenge to relational databases. Recently many enterprises have begun to develop systems of NoSQL, and NoSQL may be referred to as "No SQL" or "Not Only SQL." In my opinion, the latter is better, for we cannot deny SQL. The problem we intend to solve is the scale of data, for a database is a single machine system in essence, and its nature of being a single machine system won't be changed even if sharding is created. As a single machine system, its scale of data and solving ability have certain limits, and to boost the scale of data and solving ability, you have to choose better servers-minicomputer, midrange, and mainframe computer. Its cost will be hundreds of times higher while its performance does not increase accordingly. Therefore it provides very poor value for money. The data scale of Taobao has come across such a bottleneck.

To break this bottleneck, the distributed system can be considered as a choice. Its large-scale application was originally started by Google. However, there is a difference between our demand and that of Google: some web pages cannot be searched by the search engine and perhaps it is slow in searching some web pages. Since Taobao is engaged in e-commerce, users' goods and transactions can't be missed or mistaken, and web pages should be displayed as fast as possible, so we need higher data consistency as well as a database with a higher access speed.

Therefore, the problem we need to solve is to provide data storage and access service with a high capacity, low cost, high consistency, and high reliability, under the condition that the data scale of Taobao is increasingly growing.

Ziliu: Generally speaking, what leads to the constraints on the data scale of traditional relational databases?

Zhengxiang: The root cause of a limited data scale of relational databases lies in the fact that the current relational databases are a single machine system in essence despite their ability to be extended in various forms.

Ziliu: When did the development of OceanBase finish? How is its application at present?

Zhengxiang: We cannot say its development has been completed, because this system needs to be continuously developed. Our development was commenced in May 2010 and the first version was released in February 2011. It has been applied to five to six systems now, and the earliest application was on the Favorites. It now has 6.3 billion pieces of records and 3 TB data, with its visitor traffic doubling that of half a year ago. Those systems which used to apply Oracle can now switch to OceanBase.

Ziliu: Competitors have the following opinions towards OceanBase:

- There is a central point. Single points will suffer from risks in case of a huge quantity of data;
- As a kind of HBase open-source software led by big companies, it has avoided many pitfalls.

What's your opinion?

Zhengxiang: The best point of OceanBase is that it has good consistency between matters and data. HBase has an edge in data capacity, with potential of millions of billions of bytes, but it doesn't solve the problem which matters. In terms of the data scale, although there is a single point (with hot standby), the data scale of OceanBase can be dozens and even hundreds of times larger than that of relational databases.

Ziliu: Is OceanBase costly?

Zhengxiang: Various teams at Taobao provide support for the promotion and application of OceanBase, e.g., the DBA team has integrated itself with OceanBase and OPS spared no effort in the process. What is vital is that OceanBase gets great support from the application and business teams. Database migration requires some workload and is under risks as well. With the coordination of the application department, OceanBase has realized seamless migration to a new platform from the original relational database platform without the need to stop providing services, and it can still continuously operate in the process of being upgraded. To date, it has been working for half a year, and its system still maintains a stable state without discontinuing its services.

Ziliu: How much cost has been saved since OceanBase was put into operation?

Zhengxiang: Actually we have not made accurate calculations about it, but first of all, it is certain that we have saved the cost for a License of Oracle (which is very high), and the number of servers has been reduced. Take the Favorites for example: originally there were 16 machines in each machine room. As OceanBase went live, there were 14 machines, but the number remained unchanged despite the data volume and page view had doubled. Currently we are replacing them with 6 machines supported by solid state discs, which are expected to provide greater page views.

In addition, such equipment is not the only stuff that costs up the most. Just as high is the cost of the network bandwidth and the racks in machine rooms. The coat in this respect will be reduced if the number of machines is reduced. The business volume of Taobao is growing rapidly, and its data volume and page views are also increasing at an accelerated pace. However, it's impossible for the resources of electric power and machine rooms to be synchronously increased. From now on, as we make efforts in enhancing our service capability and performance, we must also reduce the number of servers. Otherwise, the cost will be too high for us to afford, and it will also be difficult for us to get the necessary machine rooms and racks. What's more, from the perspective of energy saving, we must conduct our operation in a low-carbon and environmently-friendly way.

Ziliu: In your previous experiences, you kept getting exceptional promotions. What do you think was the main reason for that?

Zhengxiang: I was lucky enough and had good opportunities. Except for living (as I am a light sleeper), I have very few demands for food and clothing in life. I am a person who is willing to answer the Communist Party of China's calls (though I am not a member of the CPC), and I am very lucky, and met some very outstanding teachers (like Mr. Wang Xuan). If you stand on the shoulders of a giant, you will make yourself outstanding as long as you make some effort. May be that's the very reason for what I've achieved.

Ziliu: Can you give some suggestions for the growth of young technicians based on your own experience?

Zhengxiang: Maybe you have often heard a saying that young people seldom have their foot on the ground, but there are many excellent young people in the place where I work, who are very intelligent, diligent, ambitious, and open-minded. It is very natural for young colleagues to seek to earn more money and get higher professional titles. In this regard, I couldn't agree more with Jack Ma—his theory is that to start a business is to make profits, but to make profits is never the first goal of Alibaba, because as long as we provide good services for our customers and after our customers make profits, we will get what we deserve for our efforts. And the truth is also applicable to one's development, i.e. if one regards making a career as his main goal, he will certainly be rewarded what he deserves, while if one regards promotion as his main goal, the result of the same thing will be completely different. In a word, your attitude ultimately determines your altitude.

Ziliu: As a student of the academician Wang Xuan when you studied in Peking University, what kind of influence did Mr. Wang have on you?

Zhengxiang: I was lucky enough to be a student of Mr. Wang and he has had a great influence on me. Broad-minded, Mr. Wang is the greatest person I have ever met. During the 13 years when I was studying and working under his instruction, I learned a lot from him (it is a pity that I failed to learn more for my lack of perception and ability). Then there were only 20+ people at our institute, so he gave each of us a lot of direction. Mr. Wang and his wife Chen Kunqiu did a considerable amount of research at the preliminary stage, upon which our team was able to make our well-known achievements. And today the simple belief to do something well has been firmly rooted in my mind, which is exactly from the influence of Mr. Wang.

Ziliu: In addition to Mr. Wang, who has influenced you most in the field of technology?

Zhengxiang: There is no other person like Mr. Wang. He is so extraordinary that no one else has ever exerted as great an influence as he has on me.

Ziliu: Since you have worked in four major enterprises including Lenovo, Microsoft, Baidu, and Taobao, can you introduce your main obtainment from each of them?

Zhengxiang: Before I left the Founder Group of Peking University, I had worked there for more than ten years under the instruction of Mr. Wang Xuan. At that time, Founder did well in technology but poor in management while Lenovo was an enterprise with good management, so I joined Lenovo to develop wireless projectors; also, I wanted to learn about how Lenovo ran itself. I worked there for almost three years and regarded storage as my new project and research interest in the next stage after the completion of wireless projectors. Then I came across Google's GFS (Google File System), but there was a faint possibility that I could switch to this area because there was a big difference between cloud computing and PCs, the primary business of Lenovo. Therefore, I joined Microsoft Research, but after I had worked there for some time, I found there were many obstacles to the application of my research achievements on the core products of Microsoft, including regional, lingual, and cultural obstacles, and it would be ideal to conduct such research in Silicon Valley or Seattle. One year later, I joined Baidu and conducted research that simply focused on BigTable (HBase was not available yet at that particular time) for more than two years. Then Baidu rebuilt its index data every week and I wanted to improve it, but after I completed the project, the research result was not applied and the project was closed.

Ziliu: What is the difference in the technical style of the above-mentioned companies?

Zhengxiang: Maybe I can only share my own opinions from my working experience—in Lenovo, the R&D personnel are required to know the market well, and participate in all the links from market demand to development, to the pilot run, and then to real mass production. Microsoft has a distinct R&D mode, in which there is a stringent process and review mechanism and each line of code needs to go through many rounds of review. Therefore Microsoft is very stable in development of products but also very slow, which is, in my opinion, one reason why it is difficult for Microsoft to develop rapidly on the Internet market. As I see it, Baidu doesn't attach as much importance as Taobao to technology, and there is a distinct KPI–driven atmosphere in Baidu, where it is difficult for different departments to cooperate with each other (in this respect Taobao is far better). There are quite many comparable things with some inessential differences which are developed by the R&D personnel of different projects at the same department or at different departments, so it appears that the individual efficiency is high but the overall efficiency is not necessarily high, which may be one reason why there is heavy overtime in Baidu.

Ziliu: You worked as a laboratory director and led a development team when you were very young, but why do you have no subordinates at Taobao?

Zhengxiang: Frankly speaking, I had no subordinates at Microsoft and Baidu as well, because my strongest point is technology development. There are many people who are better at management than I, and we should play to our strengths. Managing is not what I am good at and it is better for me to be engaged in development of technologies.

Ziliu: How do you lead a development team without any immediate subordinates?

Zhengxiang: In fact, all the work is done through the cooperation of people, and this is not a personal product of my own but of the whole team. This is an excellent team, in which Duolong has done a lot of critical work and such leaders as Dongxie, Zhengming, and Chucai as well as each member provided me with a lot of support.

Ziliu: Do you still write code at present? How do you control the fulfillment of a system to be consistent with your anticipation?

Zhengxiang: I am keen on code writing and I wrote an algorithm for data compression some time ago, but it was not applied, for we could not get an ideal result with it. Now I spend very little time writhing algorithms, but I will review the code written by other members of the team. In the past two months I have always been busy with recruitment, so there is some new code for me to review.

Ziliu: In what areas do you still want to make a breakthrough? What research methods do you use?

Zhengxiang: I am not so farsighted. However, considering the fact that the personnel engaged in GFS, MapReduce, and BigTable in Google still continue their work, I think there are still many things to do for Taobao in the field of data storage and processing. For example, our transactions are done by a single machine system at present, which can be changed into a cluster, and we are considering integrating the support of SQL language into it gradually. We have only moved a small step from the traditional database and there is still a large space for us to explore.

Ziliu: You keep a plain dressing style, which has intrigued many people's interest. Would you mind explaining the reason?

Zhengxiang: In fact, I was born poor and suffered from hunger during my childhood. Some of my buddies in my younger days are still struggling for living, so I am really content with what I have. I think what I get exceeds what I give to society. Instead of a deliberate act, my dressing style just indicates a poor taste, and there is no need for anyone to follow me in this respect.

Bixuan—Veteran Technical Expert of the Group's Core System

Since he joined Taobao in 2006, Bixuan has been applying OSGi to commercial products. He wrote two OpenDocs *(OSGi Practice* and *Advanced OSGi*) and one book (*Principles and Best Practices of OSGi*) which have encouraged the promotion of OSGi in China. He is now in charge of the Taobao High-Speed Service Framework which is receiving over 10 billion service requests on a daily basis. In June, 2010, he published his new work *Distributed JAVA Application: Basis and Practice.*

Bixuan is interested in Internet technologies with high availability, high concurrency, high speed, scalability, and low cost, and large distributed JAVA applications which are dynamic and modularized.

Ziliu: What about the size of your HBase clusters?

Bixuan: Now we have 15 independent HBase clusters with 20 projects running on them. These projects can store several billion pieces of data, but they haven't been able to store such a large amount as ten billion or a hundred billion pieces of data. We will soon issue a new project which can hold over a hundred billion pieces of data.

Ziliu: What are the features of Taobao HBase?

Bixuan: First of all, it is more stable, but it doesn't differ much in other respects from HBase used outside Taobao. In terms of deployment, we have improved the HBase with a set of monitoring systems and a set of things related to HBase's operation and maintenance (without which, HBase was likely to go wrong). Another feature is that Taobao HBase is more developed than the official one. It is probably because we have more applications with various usages, which required us to deal with more problems.

Ziliu: Will HBase become more complicated due to what you have done to it?

Bixuan: No, it will not. Like Facebook, we emphasize that we only use HBase for storage.

Ziliu: As a technical expert of your level, you need to promote your technologies and ideas in addition to doing your own work well. Do you meet with obstacles in such promotion?

Bixuan: In fact, when recalling our promotion of things, we see few obstacles. An obstacle is usually brought about by the conflict between things being promoted and the others. It is possible that there is someone else who is developing the same thing as you, which may lead to obstacles. For me, it is not important whether people use my products or not. What really matters is that my ideas are put into practice in spite of the fact that how such practice has been realized or who has implemented such practice.

Ziliu: It requires cooperation with many people when developing such general base products. What kind of people do you like most to work with?

Bixuan: People who can do their work well will be OK. It is fine that people agree on an idea that will bring benefit to the company or to a certain business, and work on it without thinking too much.

Ziliu: You wrote on Weibo that "Over the past four years in the company, I am proud and feel a sense of accomplishment to have done three things (one product and the promotion and application of two ideas). I am now doing the fourth one and planning the fifth." Can you tell us what these five things are?

Bixuan: The fifth one is a secret, but I can say something about the other four. The product is Taobao Auto-Publishing System. It is a low-tech system with which all JAVA systems of Taobao are published automatically. Although the product does not involve much technology, it has brought changes to Taobao, if you ask me. The development of the product was started by me, so I feel a sense of accomplishment.

The first idea is about capacity planning. We had never carried out capacity planning in Taobao. Although I didn't participate in the application of the idea, it became a product in the CSP platform anyway. I think that capacity planning is an important step for the company. The other idea is about graceful degradation which has long been talked about. People could hardly accept the idea at the beginning, but it is now applied to almost all systems. The most obvious example is that it is applied to prevent Taobao's system from catastrophic failures during sales promotions.

We are now engaging in the fourth which is to modify the entire operation and maintenance system of Taobao. Subject to some network-related factors, it is not easy to conduct expansion in Taobao. We hope to develop a set of systems that enable easy expansion so that we can conduct expansion whenever we want to. After that, we will try to increase the utilization of machines. This is the fourth thing we are doing.

Ziliu: I thought that you would talk about JAVA middleware.)

Bixuan: This is probably the product of the widest influence developed by me in the company. However, I think that it is because I was then in the position of developing the product. It would turn out to be almost the same if someone else were in the position.

Ziliu: How many technological transformations have you experienced in your work? What has resulted in these transformations? What is the main source of stress in these transformations?

Bixuan: I think that my transformations are connected with those of Taobao. When I newly joined Taobao, we had to deal with problems caused by the increasing PVs. We developed many pieces of middleware for this purpose. I was not familiar with this at that moment. (Laughs).

After solving the Drug-related problem, we came across another problem, caused by the soaring data volume. We began to think about methods for the storage, analysis, and mining of the huge amount of data. I experienced a transformation in my work then and began to do data-related work.

The main source of stress was that many people expected much of me because of my high position. However, what I had accumulated in my previous work was of little help. There were many things that I had to start from scratch when I entered a brand new field. Everyone expected me to develop a great product in a short time on account of my high position, which put me under great pressure. Things will be much better if the product developed by me after my transformation is just what the times need and has business scenarios.

Ziliu: I have learned that you were a biology major, but you are now an expert in Internet technology. How did you do that?

Bixuan: I got my bachelor's degree in biology. After graduation, I worked on systems software oriented towards the government and enterprises, which was quite different from the Internet sector. I worked in the enterprise software sector for many years and later had the opportunity to learn something about the Internet sector like Tencent technologies. These technologies came really as a revelation to us who were developing enterprise software. Developing enterprise software and Internet technologies brought different senses of accomplishment. I used to believe that Internet applications involved little technology and that anyone who worked in the technology sector could develop one easily because it was just a website. However, as I went further into Tencent technologies, I felt that it would be fine to join an Internet enterprise, and I wanted to know that how an Internet website was developed. Later, I joined WBAI, a company that ran a lottery website. I then found that it was really hard to run a website well because it involved many technologies, and I had a lot of things to learn. After leaving WBAI, I came to Taobao.

Ziliu: How much time do you spend on coding, and on learning?

Bixuan: I usually spend a lot of time reading articles and books on technology, and I spend only two or three hours on coding every day. Every once in a while I will think about the next thing to do because time flies when you are writing computer programs, which requires you to think beyond coding.

Ziliu: Is there anything that takes much time but means little to you?

Bixuan: For example, I have to attend various meetings…

Ziliu: When you taught in Taobao University of Technology, you told your students that "Do your current job well and don't worry about your future development." What do you think of promotion, as many students are struggling with this subject?

Bixuan: Everyone believes that one will get a promotion at the appropriate time. It is natural that people care about promotion. There are few people who pay no attention to their positions and therefore, suffer little pressure of life, haha. There is no solution to the problem that someone cannot get a promotion in any event. I think that the most important thing towards promotion is that you can look back on what you have done or contributed to the company, or how much you have improved in terms of technology over the last year.

For technicians, it's usually the case that you can see from the name list of promotions someone who has less technological accomplishment than yourself. Why does this person get promoted, and why it is not you? I think that whether one can be promoted depends most on how much he has contributed to the company. You may boast a high technological caliber, but you contribute nothing to the company.

Ziliu: You are a judge for the promotion of technicians in the company. When you are selecting someone, what aspects do you think are the most important?

Bixuan: If you are a technician, we will first pay attention to your technological proficiency and then, we will see how much you have contributed to the company. In addition, I will also see if you can think beyond your own responsibilities, which means that you can think of future problems that may occur and solutions to these problems. Certainly, it would be better if you could put your thinking into practice. We will focus on the problem that you have solved, regardless of how much technology your product contains. We will consider you to be important to the company if you can meet these requirements.

Ziliu: You are often invited to be an interviewer for campus recruitment. What kind of students do you appreciate?

Bixuan: In campus recruitment, I appreciate those students who do things other than studying. I always ask them if they have developed some simple programs in their spare time just because of their interest in technology. We are interested in such students because we believe that they are truly fond of technology. Students do not have to be extremely smart, and we believe that there would be nothing wrong with their intelligence as they have been admitted to a good university.

Ziliu: You are now 30 years old and have your own house and car. Also you will have a baby soon. Living such a happy life, what are you going to do next, and what is your lifelong aspiration?

Bixuan: I used to think of changing the world with technology, but it seems that I have to give up because it is really hard to realize. My current objective is to improve the company with technologies I have developed, so as to bring the company to a higher stage.

Fangweng –Head of the Taobao Open Platform Program

Fangweng joined Alibaba in March 2006, and joined the Alibaba Software Start-up Team in early 2007, responsible for the design and realization of the basic platform structure. At the end of 2007, he began to cooperate with Taobao in developing the open platform, where he was in charge of the design and realization of the system framework. In August 2009, he joined Taobao, responsible for the structure of the Taobao Open Platform.

As a Technical Expert

Ziliu: How did you develop yourself as a technical expert?

Fangweng: I have only worked with two companies since my graduation. The first one is Eastern Communications Co., Ltd (Eastcom), and the second one is Alibaba. Eastcom is a state-owned enterprise where I worked for four years and I quickly developed from a student to a supervisor of a small department. It was because my supervisors resigned one after another and I kept taking their places. In technical terms, I did make progress but it was rather modest. Four years later, I came across some bottle-necks in my development. Although it was very comfortable there, it was not a place that people of my age were meant to be. I was only about 27 years old and I wanted to have a different environment.

Then I applied for two positions in Alibaba. The first was a position in a department of the backend, but I found it was not what I wanted. Later, a concept of Ali software was proposed: work at Alibaba. I was personally interested in this idea and then I joined Alibaba. I found it was not as good as I imagined because I became a person who had to be engaged in basic coding work, and I used to have much flexibility at work. And I became a little upset. At the end of 2006, I started to play my part in the entrepreneurship of Ali software, and was enclosed in the Lakeside Garden, a neighborhood in Hangzhou. Ali purchased a company in the city of Chengdu at that time, which specialized in the development of the modeling type applications. There was less space to perform in this kind of development, compared to the Web application development that we usually did. In most cases, we just needed to build the applications of administrative software by means of XML files. The bottom layer was already packaged, which made it a lot duller than the development work these days. Then a problem emerged that there were only three people developing the core platform in the purchased company while a lot more were doing business development. However, the frame, with a lot of bugs then, was not mature enough. The business staff would propose a lot of questions and bugs to these three people of the core team. And of course, they were too busy to deal with them and many people had to wait for them to solve the problems. Out of the interest in the frame, I started to study the front end, the back end and the entire system and helped them fix some bugs. I didn't have the authority to submit the trunk so I informed them every time I had made modifications. They would review and submit them if no problem was found. After two weeks, the boss responsible for the platform invited me to join their team and therefore, I was transferred to the Platform Department. Because of my competency in this sphere and some opportunities, I began to take charge of the operation of the infrastructure and framework of the whole platform while the three above-mentioned people were still working to support business. During the four years in Ali Software after the work in Lakeside Garden, I was responsible of the development of the whole platform and the bottom structure. Therefore, I was quite ahead of others in this aspect.

Later on, we cooperated with Taobao Open platform and were transferred here. Much of what we did at that time was the very first attempt ever in the industry. Now it has been almost 4 years. We are still improving our technology.

In short, from a state-owned enterprise to a private company, it was a jump for me. I found my opportunity in the start-up team where I managed to work as a software architect. And then we kept improving this single product and now we have some technical development and influence.

Ziliu: You have been in this industry for almost 10 years. Have you had any suffering atwork?

Fangweng: There were times that I got frustrated. For example, it was hard to adjust myself when I came to Alibaba from Eastcom. And there were also a lot of trivial things when I started the work in Ali Software. I also told many newcomers that the first three to six months after you join the company will be the period of the greatest suffering. I still felt frustrated in the following period in Ali Software though others might think that this fellow was quite free, doing what he liked. It is still the same as it is now in Taobao that many of the products of the middleware teams that do not bear a close connection with business are likely to meet obstacles when applied to the business system. Faced with the obstacles, the teams, as often as not, yield to the business. Some business will require such things as white lists, black lists, or special channels. However, I have to keep the integrity and unity of those basic services.. This is when skills of coordination and communication are needed. As a software architect, I always feel frustrated as we sometimes find that what we have worked out may not be implemented. I persisted in working for the Open Platform for 4 years. And later, I had some reflections. Bixuan and I both feel that we need to find a point in business and dig further in technology to solve every problem so that the effect of the platform can be displayed. Now my role has been changed into a business architect in the business team from someone who was engaged purely in middleware and platform structures. I am now engaged in technique and business architecture.

The Open Platform is something in the middle. Some part of it depends on the back-end. Sometimes the back-end people do not care very much when I need their support and this is when we need to sit down and talk. It is all right when it is in the company with our colleagues. But when it comes to working with others, or coordinating with other departments, it is quite troublesome. This is why the technicians should develop themselves as well.

In addition, like other companies engaging in the open platform development, every department in the company wishes to work on the open platform. That whether the platform responds fast enough and whether it provides good service will affect others' decision to operate through your platform. We found that it is the same case in Baidu, Tencent, and Shanda. The open platform hopes it will be a unified open platform for the whole company, but actually, every department is doing their own open platform. Now we have become open-minded. We would rather improve our products than preventing others doing that on their own. If we make better products, these departments will naturally think that if it is worth paying that much to do that. I believe that those who deal with technical products should transfer their train of thought. It will be effective in a short term to demand others to use your products by taking administrative and compulsory measures, but in the long run, it depends on your products, and if they are qualified technology, if you have considered it from the users' perspective, or if they are simply good enough.

Ziliu: After you are promoted to the highest position on the P level, there are no other people to control your goals in terms of technology. What is your focus for the moment? How will you achieve self-fulfillment in the future?

Fangweng: In fact, I haven't had anyone doing planning for me since I reached P7. The Technology Committee defines that in the P7-P9 range that P7staff should provide directorial instruction for a small product or team, and P8 staff for a big department or a product of the company level, and for P9 staff, apart from the products of their own, they should also consider if their products will do any good to the development of the company. For me, when I am working for the Open Platform, I should not only consider the development of the platform itself but also I need to see if it will provide help for the development of other departments and the company as a whole. I persist in working on the open platform because I believe as there are so many companies which are doing this, there will be more cooperation than competition in the future. For example, if I work with Sina, they will get more Weibo users and we will obtain a higher trading volume. I want to further develop the open platform to connect with large Internet companies so that we can create more opportunities for our buyers and sellers with more resources outside.

From a technical viewpoint, I often look for breakthroughs from practical questions. If I can solve the problem, then I command the technology. In fact, I will encounter bottlenecks now. Sometimes, the technology is fast enough while the business still falls behind. Many technical employees will feel confused. I shall think about more things. For example, we are doing TQL and long-lived data push and so on. When we make significant technological innovations, we will also create a great influence in the industry. But from the client's perspective, we will have to promote in some way. I will spend some time and energy in schools and ISV to promote some of our good products next year.

Ziliu: What achievements have you made in the open platform?

Fangweng: Seeing from the big promotion on Double 11, 95% of those sellers on Taobao Mall (now known as Tmall) and the big sellers in Taobao Market have connected to the platform. The difference between connecting to the platform and otherwise is up to 90%, judging from the practical effect. It means that the gap between their speed of dealing with the order, delivering, or returning is quite large. We have made great contributions to the ERP system of big sellers. In addition, we are doing more in such aspects as the shopping guide in different categories, furnishing market, mobile Taobao, as well as the combination with systems like Sina and Meilishuo. The whole system is opening gradually.

Ziliu: Tencent and Sina are also doing open platforms. What is the relationship between them and Taobao?

Fangweng: For ordinary products on the Internet, the more we do, the fiercer the competition gets. But it is not the case with the open platform. The more we do, the more sophisticated the system will be. For instance, if we cooperate with Sina, both of us will get what we want. They need users' information and activity and we need trading. Like Facebook, Sina doesn't want anything but users. They do not care anything generated after they use the platform, e.g. buying things or playing games. What they care is that the users are using their platform. And this means the platform is successful.

Ziliu: You have been promoted to the level of "Senior Grand Tutor"[2] in Taobao Technology University. Where does your motivation of teaching come from?

Fangweng: The biggest motivation is that I hope the open platform will be a platform that supports the development of Taobao in the next 3 to 5 years. Such a platform cannot be finished by one single department. I hope I can spread this conception to more people by means of the Technology University. When anyone wants to do something, he will know that there is such a platform.

Ziliu: Your sharing with the engineers has received a good response. What kind of sharing do you think can touch the engineers?

Fangweng: There are two points. The main concern of the technical staff is whether the technology is good enough. If it is not, they will feel the lessons are a little exaggerated no matter how well you speak. So every time I just talk about something about technology, not something specific to realize the details but rather some universal

---

[2] The tutors in Taobao Technology University rank from Tutor, Mentor, Master, Great Master to Senior Grand Tutor.

methods and concepts. The other point is my belief and conception of the platform—what I can do for Taobao through this platform. By this, the audience will find the lesson helpful.

Ziliu: What are your requirements for newcomers?

Fangweng: First, they should think on their own before asking others for help when encountering troubles. Second, they should continuously break down their ideas. They should not be afraid to start over again even when 50% of the work has been done. The two newcomers I am training have now experienced very fast growth. Both of them have had similar experiences in that something they did I repeatedly denied. They have grown quickly in this period, as they had to think why I asked them to start all over. If they could not figure out the reason, it would be more likely for them to repeat it again next time. And they gradually learned to think independently.

Ziliu: Do you have any advice for the engineers?

Fangweng: Not a single company can assure absolute fairness, no matter what measures it adopts. At the end, only a small number of people will get the opportunity. It is useless to complain or feel angry about it. You have to continuously strive for your opportunity.

As a Father

Ziliu: Your child is now 2 and a half years old. How has your life been changed after you became a father?

Fangweng: There are great limitations on my time. My lifestyle has also changed. I used to do sports in the morning and sleep early at night. Now I seldom sleep before 12 and I do less sports. Some of my time after work has to be spent on my child. I can only do my own things after he has fallen asleep.

Ziliu: How is your mentality changed after you become a father?

Fangweng: After my child was born, I found that raising a child takes much patience. Little babies often make trouble out of nothing, but we cannot argue with them, but we have cope properly with them. My mentality has become very good, which is beneficial to my work. But my change in this aspect is not enough. With my family, my work has a different meaning. I will have to shoulder a greater responsibility for my family and therefore I have greater demands on myself.

Ziliu: What do you expect of your child's future?

Fangweng: Not too much. I hope he will be healthy and he can do whatever he likes when he grows up. (Will you recommend him to work in our industry?) It depends on him. If he likes, I will support him. If he likes something else, my support for him will be none the less.

Ziliu: You also treat TOP as your child. What kind of mentality is this?

Fangweng: The Open Platform is about the same age as my child. We should treat our products as if they were our children. We won't abandon them after giving birth to them but instead we have to be responsible for their development. No matter what shortcomings the child has, bad temper or poor health, we have the responsibility to take care of his growth and to solve his problems. We should not watch everything that happens as an onlooker.

As the Husband of a Beauty

Ziliu: As a tech geek, how did you attract your wife?

Fangweng: It was quite an odd thing that I met my wife and got married. How come? When I was working at Eastcom, someone tried to make match for me and introduced a girl for me. She was the classmate of a girl who helped to arrange for me. But I did not like this classmate and refused her. Later, I found I liked this girl who arranged this for me more and more, and then... My wife is good tempered. I like her very much. She feels that I am honest and reliable.

Ziliu: You are so busy with work. There will be less time for the family. How do you balance your work and personal life?

Fangweng: My father and mother will help look after my child, so they relieved a lot of my pressure. I do not want them to be too weary in the evening. So I will take care of my son for about one hour in the evening. And at the weekend, I will spare one day with him.

Ziliu: Your wife is an Internet-shopping pioneer. What role have you played in this?

Fangweng: In fact, before I Joined Alibaba, I helped my wife start her shop (in 2006) and delivered goods for her. And later we closed it. She is better at this than I am. I do not need to play any role in this, as she is familiar with online shopping herself. (Do you go against her buying too many things?) Actually, I am quite OK when she buys her own things. But if she buys something for our home, I will sometimes oppose her, as our apartment is not so big and too many things will occupy the space.

Colorful Leisure Time

Ziliu: You are very good at singing in a KTV, but are also fond of outdoor sports, which is different from other geeks.

Fangweng: When I was at school, there were not so many entertaining activities as today. There was a small KTV near our school where we could book a small table with RMB 15. You can have tea and sing at that table and there were many such tables around. When you finished a song, others applauded. It was a nice feeling. Many programmers prefer to stay at home. I think we'd better do some outdoor sports or sing a bit when the weather is not so nice. Both activities will soothe you and relieve your pressure.

Ziliu: Now that you have a happy family and a good career. What is your life pursuit in the future?

Fangweng: I once said that if I left Taobao one day, I would choose a small company or a start-up team and develop something from the beginning. Like this, I would have experienced everything, and I would have been satisfied. After this, I hope I can tour around the world and make my life a perfect one.

Wu Hanqing—Senior Security Expert of the Information Security Center of Aliyun

Wu Hanqing, who is nicknamed Xiaohei, graduated from the Special Class for Gifted Youth of Xi'an Jiaotong University. He began to study computer attack and defence techniques in 2000. During his college years, he founded the "Phantom Troupe," which has had a great impact in the web security circles in China. In 2009, he joined Alibaba Cloud Computing Ltd. and was in charge of cloud computing security and fighting against Internet fraud. He has become one of the most valuable security experts in Alibaba. He is the author of *Web Security: From a White Hat Perspective*, which is the authoritative book on Internet security.

Ziliu: The first thing that occurs to me when I meet a security expert is about computer security. Can antivirus software ensure the client security?

Wu Hanqing: It seems that antivirus software has become a necessity for PCs. However, the antivirus software can only make your

PC "seemingly safe," and it is very difficult to ensure real computer security. Such rampant viruses as the TrojanHorse are mainly designed against antivirus software. Before they make an attack on your computer, they may first check out whether they have evaded the detection of antivirus software like 360, Norton, and McAfee.

Ziliu: Many Internet security problems have sprung up in recent years. Companies are extremely fearful of security problems, which can be fatal to them. In your opinion, how much does it cost for a company to ensure Internet security?

Wu Hanqing: Internet security is essential to business growth. However, the cost of Internet security as a proportion of the total cost of business operations should not be increased blindly, and a company should deal with the most urgent matters first. The cost of Internet security varies in different sectors. Sectors such as those selling counterfeit medicine or running private online game servers are vulnerable to attacks by competitors; while non-profit sectors like those running regional BBS are less likely to be attacked. Therefore, the cost of Internet security depends on which sector you engage in and the size of your business. Investment in security includes many aspects, such as personnel recruitment, equipment, and security services purchase, and security assessment.

Ziliu: Considering that we are facing a shortage of Internet security professionals, are there any "cloud security" services similar to cloud storage?

Wu Hanqing: At present, most webmasters who use Aliyun are persons maintaining small or medium-sized websites. They don't have much money to invest in maintaining Internet security. However, equipment used for this purpose is expensive. For example, the cheapest equipment for defending against DDoS attacks costs hundreds of thousands RMB. It is not worthwhile to spend such a big amount, which might be equal to the annual profit of the websites. The advantage of cloud computing is that it can divide resources into small parts and provide resources on demand. For example, if you use cloud security, we will help you deal with attacks and charge you according to the number of attacks. The cost is thus decreased and you may only need to spend several thousand yuan on dealing with attacks. We have made security services cost-efficient.

Ziliu: Does every hacker have the experience of being a "black hat" before he becomes a "white hat"? (a white hat is an ethical hacker while a black hat is malicious.)

Wu Hanqing: I know little about today's hackers. Hackers of our times have more or less attacked or broken into some websites. What matters is that why did you break into the websites. We found it acceptable if you broke security for non-malicious reasons such as finding vulnerabilities of the website or testing new technologies. (Such practices are now prohibited by an amendment to Chinese criminal law, and we suggest people not break security for any reason.) Some hackers are motivated by profit and they might be involved in black industry chains. They are not always proficient in hacking techniques, and some of them steal a person's password by first gaining his trust through cheating and then sending him a Trojan. It is a trick rather than a hacking technique.

We are very careful when recruiting new members. We would like to know their previous working experiences, and we won't recruit those who were black hats.

Ziliu: A few years ago, there was an online battle between Chinese and American hackers. Hackers attacked not merely websites that sold bear bile, but also sites that sold good medicine. Did you participate in these activities?

Wu Hanqing: Now I do not pay much attention to this sort of things. There are some young people whose behaviours are motivated by emotions, and they cannot help breaking into such websites. It is not because they are proficient, but because the websites have done poorly in maintaining security.

Ziliu: Have you ever participated in any contests between white hats and black hats since you joined Alibaba?

Wu Hanqing: Many people might think that the contest between white and black hats is pretty cool. Some films might be misleading, while the contest in real life is quite simple. It is always the case that I have had my website well protected when someone attacks it. If he can not break into the website, he will leave directly; or he might see something about the website before he leaves. There were friends who informed us of the vulnerabilities in our websites. In addition, security teams in different Internet companies always communicate with each other, and we will also tell Tencent and Baidu if there are vulnerabilities in their websites.

Hackers who are involved in black industry chains have bothered us most, especially those doing phishing scams. They are, actually, not real hackers because they attack websites by taking advantage of vulnerabilities or using Trojans, which is a combination of real attacks and fraud. I have been engaged in dealing with such issues in order to reduce security problems of Taobao and Alipay. In the past, a phishing website could survive for half a month with no one noticing it. At present, we can detect it within several minutes after it appears, and we can even shut down a phishing website once it sends its link at Wangwang. A phisher can use the trick only once.

Ziliu: Are there any black hats who have high-level skills in hacking and bring you much trouble?

Wu Hanqing: There are very few of them. Black hats have limited career choices. They either work for large Internet companies or security companies that make security software, or they might be recruited by the national information security team to protect the national network and information security.

Ziliu: Are there any creeds or principles for white hat hackers?

Wu Hanqing: First, we shall abide by the hacker ethic; and second, we must assume everyone to be a potential black hat, and we cannot even fully trust in the person who is one of us. Everyone's operation is recorded and examined through technological means, and one's permissions to servers are revoked after the operation. In fact, few of us have the access rights to servers, so as to ensure that we cannot hack the websites of our own company.

Ziliu: In *Web Security: From a White Hat Perspective*, you showed many examples about attacks and defence. Are you worried that there would be someone who does something bad after studying these examples?

Wu Hanqing: Every coin has two sides. On one hand, what I have written is available on the Internet and the references that I have used can be found online. One can easily find such information on the Internet if he wants to do something bad by using the information. On the other hand, the reason why the open-source software is more secure is that its source code is publicly accessible, which is the same with hacking techniques. You know how to attack, as well as how to defence, because both the attack and defence techniques are made available to you.

Ziliu: Whenever a new technology is developed, there will be someone who seeks vulnerabilities in it and attacks on the vulnerabilities. It seems that the attack and the defence are two basic practices in the natural ecosystem, and what about the cyber ecosystem, is it a balanced ecosystem?

Wu Hanqing: There will always be new security problems as the technology develops, and we should find new ways to resolve them. This is a process of achieving a balanced cyber ecosystem, just like how the natural one does. The one who breaks security only needs to seek one or two vulnerabilities; while the one who defences against such attacks has to find out all vulnerabilities and remove them. Is it hard to do so? It is hard indeed. Sometimes you need to track the person that performs attacks and study the vulnerabilities that he is interested in. For example, if a black hat is studying a certain kind of cell phone recently, then you should study the same kind of cell phone, too. If the black hat turns to cloud computing later, you should turn your attention to cloud computing as well. What's more, you must study the cell phone or cloud computing more thoroughly than the black hat does, so as to remove the vulnerabilities before he performs an attack.

Ziliu: You are a backend developer, and people think of you only when the system goes wrong. Where does your sense of accomplishment come from, and how do you evaluate your performance?

Wu Hanqing: We had long been bothered with the problem of how to quantify security issues. We introduced a system later to make security concerns part of the software development process. Everyone participating in the process must learn about Internet security. We told them what they could do and what they couldn't, and thus they knew our existence. We can also quantify security issues through dealing with the following questions, including how many security vulnerabilities that we have found out today, whether or not the number of the vulnerabilities will decrease in the next month, and whether the developers have improved their code?

Our sense of accomplishment mainly comes from two sources: one is that the company's products become better and better; the other is that we have overcome some technical difficulties in our work. The latter can be purely counted as a sense of accomplishment in technical terms.

Ziliu: After you have presented a complete set of Internet security solutions, you still need many departments and people to implement the solutions. How do you promote your security technologies?

Wu Hanqing: We have developed an approach called SDL (security development lifecycle), and its implementation depends on the degree of maturity of the company's software engineering. It becomes easier to practise the approach as the company's software engineering gets more developed. We have gained some successful experience in implementing the approach in the B2B field. The SQA can ensure that every link in the lifecycle meets desired quality measures, and we only need to tell SQA what to do at every link. Development processes in some other companies are a bit confusing, and it is hard for us to promote our security technologies. Therefore, we will have all their engineers trained and tell them what to do at every link. What' more, the software must be signed for approval by a software security engineer before it is released.

Ziliu: You went to the Special Class for Gifted Youth at university and became the youngest expert in Alibaba (becoming a security expert at 23). It seems to others that you are a genius. What do you think of your experiences?

Wu Hanqing: I think that we should be patient in terms of success. Many of my former classmates in the special class are not doing well. When I was in the special class, all the fellow students were older than me, and I even couldn't find a girlfriend (laughs). Students of that age could not control their emotions and behaviours. Therefore, it was hard for them to resist the temptation to hang out after they entered university, which was not good for them. I went to the special class because my parents wanted me to. However, I joined Alibaba and have been engaged in computer security because I am interested in it. It is not about success but interest.

Ziliu: You said in your book that when you came to Alibaba for an interview, the interviewer asked you to show your technological proficiency, and you hacked the company's office network. How did you do that?

Wu Hanqing: It was not the intranet of the company, but the network for handling office work. My friends and I had basically controlled the company's networks in Zhejiang, most of which were telecommunication networks.

Ziliu: Can you give some advice for technicians who have recently entered the computer security sector?

Wu Hanqing: First, you should strengthen your basic skills. You need to study common vulnerabilities, which means to seek and analyze these vulnerabilities. Do remember not to do bad things with such vulnerabilities. Second, you can study some open vulnerabilities and see how to exploit them.

Yunzheng—Veteran Technical Expert of Data Platform and Product Department

Zhang Qing, nicknamed Yunzheng in Taobao, graduated from the Computer Science Department of Zhejiang University in 2002 and joined Alibaba in early 2003. He successfully created Alibaba DW (Data Warehouse) and witnessed the mature application of Alibaba DW from its creation. When Taobao data was launched in 2005, he was transferred to Taobao to build a Taobao data platform system to drive the construction of its commercial intelligent system. He has a penchant for the latest data technologies at home and abroad. In his communication with the Chinese and foreigin experts of the industry and from his practice at Alibaba and Taobao, he integrates what he has learned and seen in his work and highlights the actual effect, without being restricted to a specific school, and has independently developed a set of practical methods of the construction and application of Taobao's data system.

Ziliu: Congratulations on your being elected as new president of the Data Branch of Taobao Technical Committee. What are some of the work plans of the Data Branch for this year?

Yunzheng: An important task for this year (2012) is to respond to the voice of the members in the branch – what's the purpose of joining the branch? Just for writing Job Models and participating in promotion review? Of course these are not enough, and what's important is to find a guide for them, increasing their sense of direction. Since there are many modules in the data field, we should not confine ourselves to a small area after working in this particular sphere for several years, and it is necessary to communicate with each other and make ourselves open-minded.

The second task is to study the new trends of data technologies, which is a routine task of every year. The range of our communication will be wider and wider, and of a more and more in-depth nature.

The third task is to exchange data within the whole group. There are many teams engaged in data research in the group, such as B2B, Alipay, Aliyun, Ali Finance and Taobao, so the strength is splintered, and now it is necessary to coordinate the teams and form a resulting force, and each company will foster its advantageous areas. If we consolidate our strengths together, the vantage point that Alibaba Group has gained in the sphere of data will not be given away to any competitor.

Ziliu: The data platform of Taobao was developed by you from the very start. Can you introduce the development process of the department?

Yunzheng: It was a department engaged in data analysis when I joined it, and then several of my colleagues, including Tianhong and Xiaolongnv, were responsible for data analysis and Zhengde, I, and several other engineers provided support to conduct database research and build a data warehouse. We began with technology development according to our customers' demands, for we put business first instead of technology. We used Oracle on a single machine at first, and later several engineers were reassigned to Qigong's team for organization restructuring, from which it began to be developed in a standardized manner, from the Oracle on a single machine to 4 to 16 and finally to 20 nodes. The number of 20 has been the limit of the Oracle cluster to date, and it has been the biggest Oracle cluster in the world (that of US Amazon only has 17 nodes). By the time we also found we had used commercial tools to their limit, and what should we do in the next step? We had no choice but to do a complete change and replace Oracle gradually, and we have accomplished this.

Ziliu: What's the difference between it and replacing Oracle on the foreground?

Yunzheng: There are many complicated types of business on the platform and its data are transferred from the foreground. The environment we face is a constantly changing one, so is the environment of the foreground, and the one it would be shifted to was the Hadoop platform, which was not familiar to us. There were three variables changing simultaneously, and our work would be easier if one of them could be controlled unchanged. For example, we could make a difference after the change of the foreground was completed, which was not allowed by the continuous operation of businesses, for we had a very high demand for timeliness. Take the program of Wucaishi for example: on the same day when the foreground went online, we went online, because we must keep the same pace with it. And we visited some of the top 500 global enterprises in the telecommunication and finance industries, finding that when they transform their foreground business, the work for background data was all suspended and the work wouldn't be started until the foreground work was delivered. Why did we do them synchronously? It was not feasible. We had no choice but to think about how to solve the problem, and we managed to solve it successfully, which had not been done by anyone else, thus being a valuable experience.

With the success of such creative work, the whole team boosted their abilities to cope with some tricky problems and they wouldn't be afraid of any new troubles but firmly believe that they would find a solution. And there is a matter worth mentioning in the process of its development—its merger with the business of Alimama. Alimama is an independent company, with a complete system from its foreground to background, and its front end needed to be linked to Taobao and all the back-end data needed to be merged. The merger involved complicated details but it was successful at last, and two products of Quantum Statistics and Data Cube were formed and the system of the back-end data was integrated into a cluster of Hadoop. Then there were four or five clusters in Alibaba, which resulted in low timeliness and a high cost of operation and maintenance. After it was integrated into a cluster, unified management, transfer, maintenance, and monitoring began to be adopted, so there were gradually fewer and fewer alarms and we were able to focus on doing business and perfecting the platform. This was a critical piece of work at that time and also a big matter we completed by gathering our strengths.

As the saying goes, "This world will separate after a long time of unification, and also will do the opposite after a long time of splitting." In the recent years, we have hatched some teams and products, which have been assigned to various subsidiaries. In 2012 we will form an official organization with Aliyun within the range of the group to lead the mode creation of "First Data Sharing Platform," namely the current project of Binghuoniao. The project comprises the two biggest data systems – Feitian and Hadoop – in the group, and the project team is composed of almost all the engineers of high level and core architects. It is a significant feat to achieve by gathering our talents together. Therefore I believe that dozens of data technical experts who are more competent and have a bigger picture in their mind will spring up from the project.

Ziliu: What benefits have been brought by the data platform through the input over the past few years?

Yunzheng: The simplest assessment method is whether these data have been turned into value, and Data Cubic and Quantum Statistics are the two products which can turn data into profit. And both of them have already brought considerable revenue. However, its value is more than the money we earn through it, for they are just our attempts in exploring the value of data and we cannot predict its future yet, whose value in the future may be beyond measure.

Ziliu: What's the difference between your data computing platform and those of Google and Amazon?

Yunzheng: As for the similarity, the data of the companies of such a grade are all distributed on a macro level. Google, which started earlier, has developed Bigtable and GFS as well as a series of products from distributed storage to distributed computing, which have already been applied to its search service. Unlike Google, Amazon provides OPS for others in the form of virtual machine and conducts cloud computing in the form of virtual machine rental, with some of its business data put on it.

Taobao builds such platforms as Yunti and Feitian by means of Patch on an open-source distributed platform. The concept of the distributed pattern is universal and we possess the intellectual property right of the whole "Feitian" system and many smart designs, and thus have great potential for independent design.

Another important difference is that the data inside are different, so is the value of the data. In the database of Taobao, you can find almost all the data about China's e-commerce from its origin to the present, including such data of goods as B2B, B2C, and C2C as well as the data for transactions and payment. On the other hand, Amazon only has B2C data and there is only searching information but no commercial data in the Google database. The data of Taobao is enormous, with a high quality, and more adaptable to the situation of China, for all of them represent the consumption habits of the Chinese people. It is necessary to continuously innovate and in a greater ecological chain to identify and explore its value.

Ziliu: What scale has your data reached at present?

Yunzheng: Our data sees an increase of 100 TB or so every day, so we are controlling the trend of a great net increase through some innovative technical methods such as limit storage.

Ziliu: As a veteran of Internet technologies, can you share with us something about your growth?

Yunzheng: In a word, it is idealism, interest, and perseverance. I have always made every endeavor to realize my dream without any time and opportunity wasted ever since I set a direction for my career, regardless of unfavorable circumstances or adversity.

I was keen on data from the time that I joined Alibaba. Another reason is that, at the early stage of the establishment of Alibaba, Jack Ma invited a former leading scientist of Amazon, Dr. Andreas Weigend, to introduce the value and importance of data to the employees of the company. Although I failed to make a good sense of it then, I stuck with it and carried on. With the development of the company from B2B DW to the data platform of Taobao, I have been lucky enough to witness the development of the data system from the conception of the Feitian system to its realization together with Aliyun since its establishment. My continuous development can owe itself not only to opportunities but also to my constant perseverance, and what makes me appreciative is that we have a group of core data technicians who have grown and matured in this environment.

Ziliu: Since you joined Alibaba in 2003, including the 9 years you worked on technical posts (till 2012), how many transfers required by the company or by yourself have you experienced? What's your opinion of these transfers?

Yunzheng: As for transfer from DBA to DW, it may be because there was no suitable person when the company began to launch its data project and then the post most relevant to data should be DBA. Therefore, I was lucky enough to be transferred to the project team and commenced the building of the first stage of the Alibaba data warehouse.

The second is the transfer to Taobao from B2B, which was in the second half of 2005 and also my voluntary choice. At that time, on the one hand, the data warehouse of B2B had been put into operation, with its basic structure completed, business had been put on a normal development track, and I had become a core member while building the B2B data warehouse, which was basically unchallenging to me. But the business of Taobao had changed greatly, and judging from industrial experiences, to build a data warehouse was under a great risk of failure and moreover is a difficult thing to do, so I decided to join Taobao to start from scratch.

The data of Taobao has always been growing rapidly and its business is constantly changing. It is such an environment that has driven the fast development of the data platform. With the major restructuring, splitting, and merger of the foreground of Taobao for several times, there are basically some unprecedented problems and challenges plaguing the data every year but all of them were successfully resolved. With the success of Taobao's Wucaishi project and the completion of the merger between the advertisement data platform and the data platform, business began to boom, which in turn became the primary driving force for the data application platform, and in this period technology and business saw a rapid growth.

When it comes to my opinion about these shifts, as I have always been a person who welcomes challenges, for I believe shifts are beneficial to a person's development and allows one to experience more. Sometimes we should even actively change our life. Should we stop seeking new breakthroughs when the platform is stable and the system begins to run on a normal track? Of course not. Instead we should set higher requirements and goals from a deeper and more comprehensive angle and try our best to realize them.

Ziliu: Could you give some suggestions to novice technicians for their career development?

Yunzheng: Your interest is the best guide for you and perseverance is the only path which can lead you to your goal. Of course, it is important to have an appropriate mentor at different stages of your development and it will be easier for you to reach your goal by setting a right direction, just as the saying goes, "A stitch in time saves nine." There are two elements which can help you set your direction when you haven't formed your own judgement at the beginning of your work, one is your interest, and the other is to find a person who you admire very much and is capable of assisting you in deciding your future direction. And of course, if the two aspects happen to overlap, what you need to do is to persevere, with your feet on the ground.

Xiaoma—Senior Technical Expert of Taobao UED Front End Common Platform

Zhao Zexin, nicknamed Xiaoma, joined Taobao in October 2006. Before that, he mainly worked in start-up companies, participating in multiple projects and playing different roles, including product developer, presale consultant, after-sale supporter, and customer training provider. After he joined Taobao and became the first front-end engineer of the whole website, he participated in the front-end development of some important products, such as Wangpu, Favorites, logistics, WebWangwang and P4P, and systematically restructured the front end of the whole transaction process of Taobao. He successively led the development of TBra, the original front-end JavaScript framework, organized a virtual team to optimize the front-end performance of each key webpage of Taobao, and was in charge of the Velocity Group of the Technical Committee. In 2010 he began to lead the front-end restructuring team, being responsible for the development and generalization of front-end general framework, support of UPC core business and the building of the front-end quality assurance system, and has translated some classic works, including JavaScript: The Good Parts.

Ziliu: As a main original initiator of the D2 Front-end Technology Forum (D2), what was your original intention to start D2? How were things going at the beginning?

Xiaoma: At that time we were in such an environment that the fraternity of front-end personnel was larger and larger and the industry became increasingly mature, but there were very few conferences for the front-end practitioners, so we intended to organize an activity for these people to communicate with each other. It was under this context that D2 came into being. I still remember the first session of D2, for which we only had very poor conditions including the conference venue, while we are proud of the number of its attendees of its activity at present and its popularity in the industry through its growth over the years.

Ziliu: As one of the main organizers of the ADC Technology Carnival/Taobao Technology Carnival event, could you make some comments on the current Technology Carnival and what's your expectation for it in the future?

Xiaoma: Speaking of our carnival conference, I would like to introduce some overseas conferences of such kind. For example, when I attended the Velocity Conference, what impressed me deeply was that a guest shared his opinion that we should regard performance as a kind of functionality, which reminded me that many projects attach great importance to function, and as long as function is qualified, the project will go live in haste, and the problems with performance have to be solved gradually. Such an opinion of this guest really struck a chord with me and there were also many other sentiments for which I became a warm seconder. After the conference was concluded, we had all benefited a lot from it and admired the organizer holding such an excellent event, so we began to consider introducing such a conference into China, and currently we are also the organizer of Velocity China.

As for the Technology Carnival we held, we are going to hold it again. On the conference last year, its organizer, Lingshan's team, brought together many sub-brands within a very short time and limited manpower, and the contents of what was shared on the conference were not inferior to any of those on many domestic conferences with a very high ticket price. And the quality of the first session of the conference has been recognized by our fraternity, which was completely beyond our expectations. In my opinion, therefore, the conference was very successful.

As for my expectation for it this year, we took the opportunity provided by the company to go abroad, and I was deeply impressed by the exhibition area of the foreign conference. For example, you can only find some gifts or conference materials prepared for attendees, or merely a box for collecting attendees' name cards at the exhibition stands of many domestic conferences, but I found more interactive activities at the exhibition stands of the overseas conference I attended. There were many game-like interactive activities in front of the exhibition stands for collecting the information of the attendees, which gave every attendee a nice experience and made them feel at ease, and thus I had an experience of each exhibition stand (laughs).

Therefore, I think there should be more elements for relaxing interaction at the venue for domestic conferences in addition to sharing quality contents. And I hope our Technology Carnival will allow the attendees to have more fun with technology, in addition to providing them with high-quality sharing of content. For the Technology Carnival of this session, we have rented a whole floor of space for arranging the exhibition, which is a new attempt of us to relieve each attendee of the pressure from work and offer them a relaxing experience. Such a conference composed of exciting topics and a lively and relaxing atmosphere will be a real technology carnival.

As for the future of the ADC Technology Carnival, I hope we can maintain its characteristics, adhere to our original intention, and stick to the non-commercial orientation of the conference in addition to saving resources for our company to provide the technicians of the subsidiaries of Alibaba and the companies dependent on the business chain of Alibaba with a platform, through which they can get a timely,overall picture of Alibaba. And the short-term goal of us is to build our conference into a weathervane of industry; and our long-term goal is to keep it up with the F8 conference and Google I/O in the industry.

Ziliu: As the first front-end engineer of Taobao, you are still working in this field after more than 5 years. Could you please briefly introduce the development of Taobao's front end?

Xiaoma: I can start with how the "front end" came into being, for I have some opinion of it. Take Taobao for example: at first Taobao was a community in which people posted some information for others to see. With the development of the Internet, what people needed was not only a static page but also a colorful and lively page, as well as more interactive. That is to say, there was an increasingly high demand for experience. In such a case, it was natural for interactions to become more and more complicated. The development personnel were not quite fit to do such a thing and it was required for a new specific trade to do it. In my opinion, the work of traditional development personnel is mainly orientated to machines, so they mainly thought about the questions of CPU, internal storage, and databases. In fact, it required some people who had more accurate understanding of users' demands to develop an interface for interactions between the Internet and its users. They need to know more about experience and pay more attention to people. On the other hand, there have been more and more clients over the past years and a page needs to adapt to more clients, which the traditional development personnel were not good at. For the reasons mentioned above, such a new trade was born.

After I came to Taobao, what I needed to do first was to make the webpage of Taobao interactive and present abundant information to bring customers a smoother experience. At that time, there was no such position as a "front-end engineer." I came here as a Java engineer. Then the front-end work of Taobao kicked off, and the work we did at first was to make the page interactive, and we did a lot work of

JavaScript development to make the whole page more lively, which was the situation of the front end of Taobao at its first stage.

When it entered the second stage, the business of Taobao became more and more complicated. There were more and more pages, and the workload of front-end development became increasingly great. Hence a large team was needed to handle the work. In the meantime, AJAX became popular, which changed the development mode of the whole industry. And more work needed to be completed via the front end. The team on the front end grew rapidly at this stage and it can be understood that the first stage is to make webpages interactive, while the second stage is to bring users a friendlier experience via the cooperation between the front end and the back end.

Then at the next stage, we found that there were more and more content displayed on the browser and more and more browsers emerged, such as Firefox, Chrome, and IE 6-8, which put a greater and greater load on the front end. In such a case, we were faced with problems of performance and it was necessary for us to do some frames and regulations and a lot of work of optimization.

The development modes have gradually become stable and mature recently, with the progress made in the Internet industry over the years. There are powerful frames for the work which traditional development personnel once were not good at, but they got into it rapidly. In terms of the cost of the company, the work which could be done by two trades can be completed merely by one trade. So there is a trend that it seems unnecessary to distinguish the types of work so clearly. Although there will be a trade of the front end on Taobao in the future, what it mainly engages in will be the work of architecture and overall planning.

Ziliu: Now it is very common for teams to be split or merged and the team of the front end is a typical one. What do you think of these changes?

Xiaoma: At first, there were only four or five members in our team and we just made webpages as required. With the division of the website's business, work began to be divided among us. For example, some were responsible for the front-end development of the mall, and some for the front-end development of the master website. Despite the division of work, we still belonged to the same team. Later, with the splitting of Taobao's master website, the concept of the business line was born, such as the product line and the shop line, and at that time the front-end team was split into several small ones, which dealt with different business lines. Such splitting had its pros and cons. The benefit was that it boosted a fast development of business while the down side was that there were a lot of overlapping projects caused by a lack of communication within the same trade. Just as the world will be unified after a long time of splitting, the teams were merged after a period. And just as the world will separate again after a long time of unification, it was not long before the whole company was split into several subsidiaries, and our team was also split into several parts affiliated to different subsidiaries. In my opinion, we shouldn't emphasize the significance of merger or splitting, for different organizational forms are needed for different stages.

For the current stage, we can say that the team is half split and half merged. Why? The reason is that the front-end team is split into two parts. One follows up the front-end development of business and the other is responsible for the development of general products, which guarantees an effective support for business. In addition, we are able to conduct effective management of general products, thus avoiding such problems as inconsistency between development environments and inconsistent standards.

Ziliu: Can you imagine the development direction of the front end?

Xiaoma: In my opinion, the distinction between the front end and the back end will be more and more blurred. That is to say, it is required that development engineers be able to link up the work at the front end and at the back end. I am relatively in favor of this opinion: after the progressive development of the development mode in these years, the development of the front end and the back end will be integrated in the future, and such a post will be called Web Development Engineer.

What's more, it doesn't matter what the name of the position is and what really matters is that there is an increasingly high demand for interactions and experience, and with the application of the mobile Internet, there will be more methods for interactions, such as slide interaction and shake interaction, which requires some people to do the development work in this respect and promote the development of the front-end technologies.

Ziliu: Judging only from the technical direction, is HTML5 a main trend in the future?

Xiaoma: HTML5 is more than the simple upgrade of HTML4. Instead, many people think that HTML5 is just the expressive language in the tag brackets. In fact, HTML5 is not the same as HTML4, for HTML5 includes not only the semantic tags added to HTML4, but also CSS3 and the API of a lot of new JavaScript (JS for short). Why are there such changes? In my opinion, it is not enough for HTML4 and some relevant technologies to make Web a very good development platform, but it can only enable Web to be an interface to display some content and support some simple interactions. However, the goal of HTML5 is to enable the whole Web to be a development platform indeed or to enable a browser to be a platform suitable for developing large-scale applications. As for such changes, firstly the change to the tag of HTML5 is to give it a higher level of semantization, then CSS3 enhances the items for presentation, and what's the most important is the newly-added API of JS. So now we can locally get linked to the database, use Socket, use local storage, and acquire the geographical location on the browser. A lot of the information which we needed to get from the background in the development process can be generated on a local browser at present. And that has turned the browser into a platform suitable for making large-scale applications rather than the one only for displaying some content in the past.

Now HTML5 is universally applied on the website of Taobao, which was one of the first websites in China to apply HTML5.

Ziliu: You have received a lot of support from the industry in the development process. Please describe what kind of influence the industry has exerted on you.

Xiaoma: There are three companies which have had a great influence on us.

The first one is Yahoo, from which the definition of the front-end positions derived. Then Yahoo was in its heyday, possessed many excellent technologies and talented personnel, and put forward the definition, frames and specifications of the front end the earliest. YUI, the JS frame we used originally, was created by Yahoo, many of our specifications were made by reference to theirs and we successfully solved the problems with performance by reference to the optimization scheme and tools (YSlow) provided by Yahoo. It can be said that many things of ours were made in our reference to those of Yahoo from 2007 to 2009.

The second one is Google and why has Google had so great an influence on the front end? The reason is that it is Google that changed AJAX into a very successful application in commerce. A lot of AJAX technologies are applied to its products such as Gmail and Docs, and the successful application of AJAX in Google drove many engineers at the front-end and of interaction to begin to utilize the technology, which has made the work at the front end become more prosperous.

The last one is Facebook, a company which has made a perfect mix of experience and technology.

In fact, the companies which have influenced us most are these three, which have ranked among the top in Silicon Valley.

Ziliu: Among them, two have been blocked in China (Google and Facebook websites cannot be accessed). Although many people know the blocking prevents the exchange of information, they don't know the block has also influenced the development of technology greatly. And the ability to circumvent the block is indispensable for a technician.

Xiaoma: Right. The funniest thing is that there is a Japanese idol named YUI, and for some time as long as you searched YUI, the results would be blocked.

Ziliu: Now let's turn back to the topic. What influence have you had on the industry?

Xiaoma: We have successfully promoted the front-end post to the industry to some extent through our blog, our sponsorship of D2, and some books we translated, which has helped many companies learn about the importance of the post and enabled many technicians to know that they are engaged in front-end work.

Ziliu: Since you and your team have translated several books, what experience can you share with us?

Xiaoma: The books we have translated are all about the front end, and the reason why we chose such books is that we need the technology in this respect at first and that it can promote the development of the front-end technology in China. When writing a book, you cannot be as free as writing a blog article, for it needs to be printed. It is necessary for you to be cautious and fully understand the principle behind it. It's just like reviewing what you have mastered and is therefore an excellent learning process. And I find it a good way of team building for the members of a team to write a book cooperatively, for it is necessary for all the members to exchange ideas and we can learn from, supervise, and push each other, which improved our relationship as well. So I recommend others to give it a try.

Another lesson we have learnt from writing books is that you cannot earn much money through writing. It is more of a benevolent activity but will take a lot of your time.

Ziliu: Could you talk about your personal growth and give some suggestions to those still at their startup stage?

Xiaoma: In retrospect, the period when I made the greatest progress in my work is the several years after I newly joined Taobao, for I was very simple, only thinking about how to do work well and proceeded to another after completing one task, without considering whether the business is important or the demand side is easy-going or not. There is a ten-thousand-hour rule saying that one can become mature only by practicing continuously and meet with problems continuously, which I think is very correct. Of course, you need to continuously make a summary and writing a blog article is a very good approach.

Ziliu: Now there are many people who choose to start a business, and as a technician who once started a business, what's your opinion?

Xiaoma: In my opinion, the reason why many people choose to start a business is that as the company where they work becomes larger and larger, there are a lot of restrictions of procedures and rules, which will leave a smaller and smaller space for your initiative. However, when you really start a business, you will be also faced with many restrictions, such as the problems with the tax bureau, the industrial and commercial bureau, trademark, company registration, shareholders' relations, staff management and the competition with the competitors in the industry, which is not different from working in a company in essence. So in my opinion, starting an undertaking is basically your attitude towards life, and to overcome difficulties one after another with your vigorous energy, great enthusiasm, and firm belief, which is to start an undertaking. I don't think there are essential differences between starting a business by yourself and starting an undertaking in a large company.

Of course, if you don't accept the overall orientation of the company where you work, or you don't accept the industry and you have a dream to start a new business, the company should be open enough to provide you with an opportunity to realize your dream.

The Program World of Taobao's Legendary Engineer—Duolong

Duolong is one of the founders of Taobao as well as the first programmer of of the site. He set the foundation of many important software programs of Taobao. Some people regard him as the "sweeping monk" (In *The Demi-Gods and Semi-Devils* by novelist Louis Cha, the sweeping monk is a seemingly unimpressive monk in Shaolin Temple, but is actually proficient in all kinds of Kungfu. He is the one who persuades the two villains to repent and do good.) and some say he is the "God." In Taobao, he knows both C/C ++ and the inner core of Java; he goes deep into the bottom of the technology department and at the same time he is also able to engage in the business field of a high level. He is active both in the front-end and back-end with wide and deep coverage. He is Duolong, a member of the Expert Panel of the Core System Department.

There is a popular saying among the junior technical staff: "Turn to Duolong if you have any trouble." I know this pretty well. Once our group was working on a strange problem, where an Apache server broke down for no reason. We worked on the problem for three days and did not find the reason for that. Finally we turned to Duolong for help. He found out the cause and told us in only three minutes. This "trouble-shooter in seconds" has taught me what a senior researcher is like.

I work in the department with Duolong, next to his seat where I can observe him easily and reflect from his behaviors on how he becomes a master in computer field from a non-professional (he was a major in Life Science of the Department of Biology).

Duolong told me that his accumulation of knowledge and experience can be attributed to the development of Taobao's business, where he encountered various kinds of problems. These problems urged him to continue to study various technologies to solve them and grow with Taobao. In my opinion, it is also vital that he maintain a humble attitude to technology. He always absorbs new knowledge like a sponge. For him, there is no question that doesn't deserve solving, no technology that doesn't deserving learning. Every time he learns something new, he will write a piece of code to verify. On one hand, it serves as practice and on the other hand, it helps him deepen his understanding and master the technology in a real sense.

Duolong has another feature that others may find it difficult to possess. When he indulges himself in the programming world, he will not be easily distracted by the outside. For most of the time during his day, he is writing code at his table. If he is not at his table, he must be in the toilet. I still remember the 2010 table tennis final of our company which was held in the Entertainment Center on the 10th floor of the Entrepreneurship Building, only 20 meters away from Duolong's table. The fanfares and buzzing attracted many to watch the game while only Duolong was clinging to his chair. Maybe this was the highest realm in *Kungfu Panda II* – the Inner Peace. It would be hard not to become a master with such concentration.

It has been many years since Duolong joined Alibaba in 2000. He is still writing code at the frontline. I asked him why he could keep doing this for such a long time and with such passion. He replied that it was easy because he was doing what he was fond of and that solving problems and writing code provided him with a sense of accomplishment. We once made a trip to the Lu Mountain. On our way back on the train, he was still writing code. That demonstrates how much he loves writing code.

In Taobao, many colleagues, from vice presidents to ordinary software engineers, admire and respect Duolong sincerely. This is partly due to their recognition of his technical caliber, and partly due to his silent effort and his personal charm. On the annual meeting of 2011, the video "One Year in Taobao, Dear" was moving to a lot of junior technical staff. Many engineers contributed a lot to the maintenance of the online steadiness of Taobao, which also meant they owed their family and relatives a lot. When we were watching the video, Duolong, who was sitting next to me burst into tears. I think the reason why he was so touched was that the story in the video was a reflection of his countless sleepless nights. Before 2009 when there was no such an organization called Fire Fighting Group to resolve and shoulder breakdowns in the company, Duolong had to solve the problems and shoot the troubles even if it was midnight. And those junior staff who had turned to him always said that he was at service at any time with an approachable and kind attitude and he was always willing to bear the burden of hard work. Now the Fire Fighting Group will still turn to him when they cannot solve problems and he will show up as soon as he is informed of the situation.

What attitude should a computer engineer have to conduct study and in what means? A simple piece of advice of Duolong may answer this question well—"Find out the problem, solve the problem, and do not bypass the core of the problem. Do more and you won't lose anything even if it is not your own matter. " This may be the very secret of Duolong's success. Not everyone can do this, though it seems quite easy. If you can do this, you'll have the potential to become a "Duolong".

Duolong always keeps his simple and abiding love for codes and his concentration and study on technology. Others may treat work as work but he treats it as a career—this is the programming world of Duolong.